Simple Solutions to Make Customers Feel like *Your* Supermarket is *Their* Supermarket

322 Ideas You Can Implement Today!

Dr. Russell J. Zwanka
Dr. John L. Stanton

ISBN-13: 9781710371703

First, start with passion.

Other Works by Zwanka

Ties That Bind: Inside the Extraordinary (sometimes knotty) Food Marketing Continuum

CBD Reality

A note from your professor

CBD Dreams

Public Speaking for Everyone

So, how do I do this Marketing thing?

Marketing in Today's Cuba

A Store Walk

Dr. Z's Guide to Grocery and Cooking and Cool Stuff Like That

Successfully Succinct Stage Speaking

A Marketing Manual for the Millennium

Category Management Principles

Customer Connectivity in Global Brands and Retailers

Requisite Reading for the Renaissance Retailer

Operating in the New Cuba

Food Retail Management Strategic Cases

Would You Shop Here if You Didn't Work Here?

Customers First. Profits Second.

Other Works by Stanton

Winning Marketing Strategy

Precision Target Marketing

MORE Stanton on Food Marketing

Stanton on Food Marketing

Success Leaves Clues!

Delight Me...The Ten Commandments of Customer Service

21 Trends in Food Marketing for the 21st Century

325 Ways to Make Customers Feel Like Your Supermarket Is Their Supermarket

Marketing Planning in a Total Quality Environment

Running a Supermarket, Consumer Focus Groups and *Making Niche Marketing Work* (McGraw-Hill). *This niche book was selected for the Business Week Book Club, and has been published in German, Portuguese, Thai, Hebrew, and Korean.*

About Stanton

John L. Stanton has a Ph.D. in Quantitative Methods and Marketing from Syracuse University, and been in the food industry for about 40 years. He is currently professor and previously held endowed chair in the food marketing department at Saint Joseph's University in Philadelphia. Dr. Stanton was elected to the European Retail Academy hall of Honor.

Besides academia, Dr. Stanton has also worked in the food industry. He has been Vice President of Marketing for Melitta, an international coffee company, and worked in Germany for Tengelmann, one of the world's largest food retailers (at the time) and owner of A&P in the USA. Dr. Stanton was also director of research of an advertising agency and has consulted for many nationally known food companies including Campbell Soup Company, Procter & Gamble, Acme, Kroger, Pepsi, Frito Lay, Florida Dept. of Citrus, Kellogg and others.

Dr. Stanton has spoken at many major US food association meetings and conferences including the Dairy Management Inc. (DMI), International Mass Retailers Association, National Retail Federation, National Grocers Association (NGA), Produce Marketing Association (PMA), Food Marketing Institute (FMI), National Association of Convenience stores (NACS), Institutional Food Distributors Association, Institute of Food technologists (IFT), National American Wholesale Grocers Association (now FDI), Snack Food Association, National Frozen Pizza Institute, Private Label Manufacturers Association (PLMA), Produce Marketing Association, National Pasta Association, National Confectioners Association, Biscuit and Cracker Association, Refrigerated Foods Association, and many others.

He was a Board of Directors or Advisors of many food companies including Frankford Candy Company, Herr's Foods, Premio Foods, The Philadelphia Cheesesteak Company, and David Michael flavor company. Currently on the Board of Directors of T-Pro.

Dr. Stanton has also worked with many of the commodity agriculture groups including the Florida Department of Citrus, Mushroom Council, Sweet Corn Association, Dairy Management Inc, cranberry growers of Ocean Spray, and numerous farm groups. Dr. Stanton has served as an expert and expert witness to many food and beverage companies including Whole Foods, Target, Coca Cola, Ahold, Supervalu, Boars Head, Safeway and many others.

Dr. Stanton has spoken to food associations in International Speeches and seminars include Mexico (ANTAD) Russia (Russian Fruit Juice Federation) Germany (Tengelmann, German Chocolate Association, European Fruit Juice Association), France (Monoprix), Argentina (Argentine Grocery Association, Denmark (AC Nielsen conference), Uruguay (Agri-business Congress), Taiwan (National Quality conference), Japan (Dairy convention), Singapore (Retail leadership conference), Sri Lanka (CMS), Brazil (ABRAS, APAS, HSM World Marketing Seminars), Italy (Deutsche Bank Venice conference), Poland (Posnan university program), Thailand (Fresh Food Association), Norway (AC Nielsen conference), Chile (Chilean Grocers Association), Sweden (AC Nielsen conference), Colombian (Colombia Grocers Association), Romania (RAU), Costa Rica (IICA), New Zealand (Food and Beverage Association), Finland(AC Nielsen conference), and Ireland (Northern Irish Food and Beverage Assoc., Musgrave), Czech Republic (USDA Food Show), and Estonia (Talinvest, US Embassy).

Dr. Stanton has been regularly quoted in the media. He was interviewed on Fox Business, CNN, the Today Show and was interviewed on NBC Nightly News with Tom Brokaw as well as numerous local channels. He has been quoted in most of the food marketing magazines, as well as in the print media, and has been quoted in *Forbes, Fortune, Advertising Age, Brand Week, New York Times, Wall Street Journal*, and many others. He hosted an episode of the History Channel's Modern Marvels entitled, "The History of the Supermarket."

About Dr. Z

Dr. Russell J. Zwanka is a Professor of Food Marketing, Marketing Research, Personal Selling, Marketing Strategy, Category Management, and Marketing Principles. Having spent a career in the food industry before teaching, Dr. Z conceptualized and formed the Food Marketing Concentration at Siena College; as well as the Food Marketing Track at the State University of New York at New Paltz.

Serving as the Chair of the Food Industry University Coalition (FIUC), Zwanka works with other universities teaching Food Marketing, to help educate the future of the food industry. The FIUC is made in part by the generosity of the National Grocers Association (NGA).

Dr. Z is CEO of Triple Eight Marketing, a retail consultancy-helping food organizations re-align around customer lifestyle and orientation. Dr. Z has led the merchandising, marketing, advertising, procurement, and all customer engagement areas for multiple food retail companies domestically and internationally.

Zwanka holds a Doctorate in International Business from ISM in Paris, France. He also holds a Master of Science in Management from Southern Wesleyan University, and a Bachelor of Science in Psychology from the University of South Carolina. Never stop learning….

Contents

How to Read--and use--This Book

Do you work in the supermarket industry, and like to have customers feel like your supermarket is their supermarket?

Well it's simple. Just solve their food shopping problems. And do it better than anyone else. And, while you're at it, be open 24 hours, deliver groceries within the hour, never have anything rotten on the shelf, have everything rotated perfectly, have a floor you can eat off, carry everything but don't have unproductive inventory, and don't forget to smile!

Now we know what you are thinking. "Wait a minute. That's tough to do. People have so many problems. And people don't want the same things. And there's competition out there, and they're not always being nice. How can you say, 'it's easy?' "

We didn't say it was easy. We said it was simple. If--and this a big if--you approach it in a systematic manner. We can show you how to do this. And how you can make the task manageable.

This book contains simple solutions to make customers feel like your supermarket is their supermarket. These tactics are in different categories such as singles, families with children and elderly.

But, how do you decide which ones you should use? How do you put these tactics into action?

Just follow the "Four Step Approach."* By so doing, you'll make customers feel like your supermarket is their supermarket.

But, before turning to the solutions, read the next four sections. You'll find these tactics are more than things to do to make immediate sales. They are tactics which, when integrated into an overall strategy, will cause various targeted customers to actually love your store--to reach that "holy grail of marketing" called brand advocacy. Yes, you reach brand advocacy, and your customers do your marketing for you. Think Wegmans, H E Butt, Publix, and even Ikea, Nike, and

Apple. Those who love these brands love these brands- and they cannot understand why other customers aren't shopping there- or using their products.

Most of the simple solutions we've listed are those we've noticed during store visits, scanning success practices or during interviews with supermarket executives. Even though we spent countless hours coming up with these ways, we readily acknowledge that we could have never come up with all the tactics possible for any target market. Therefore, we have also included blank forms in the back for you to create your own tactics. By the way, we would appreciate it if you could send us a copy of the tactics you add to your book. You can reach us at any of our social media sites (@rzwanka), or email (rzwanka@siena.edu, jstanton@sju.edu)

* "The Four Step Approach" is largely from an article we wrote for Supermarket Business, "Aiming for the Shoppers You Want/A Little Marketing Marksmanship," May, 1995, pp.33-42.

Four Step Approach to Target Marketing

STEP 1: EMBRACE CHANGE

The Problem: What Made Supermarkets Successful Yesterday Won't Make Supermarkets Successful Tomorrow- Or Even Today

What made supermarkets successful in the past is not going to work in the future. It's probably not even working that well today.

Everything changes. You have a traditional store, and you get beat on price. You have a price format, and you get beat on fresh. You have everyday low prices, and weekly specials are better. There's a pet supply store taking all your dog food sales....it never ends. Every good idea is taken by someone else. That's the nature of a free market economy. Be happy about that. Competition sharpens all blades.

What we're saying is the future is going to require different strategies than those that worked in the past.

It was best articulated by Peter Drucker who said, "In a fast-changing world, what worked yesterday probably doesn't work today." Walt Disney understood the importance of change when he wrote, "In this volatile business of ours, we can ill afford to rest on our laurels, even to pause in retrospect. Times and conditions change so rapidly that we must keep our aim constantly on the future."

Sometimes executives are reluctant to change because they have been successful. They argue "why change when you don't have to?". I think we can all understand that logic, but it does not mean a company shouldn't be preparing for changes to take place in the market; and therefore, they will need to adjust...even the successful firms. Malcom Forbes said the greatest obstacle to business is success.

Marketing Is a Passing Parade

Remember when you went to a parade and you got there early so you could have a great viewing point? The band passed right in front of you. As did the clowns. And the elephants. But, soon the parade passed you by. Although you had the "best seat in the house", the only thing you could see then were the backsides of the elephants fading into the distance.

Marketing's the same way. Yesterday's "best seat" is not going to be the "best seat" forever. We must move with the parade. Looking at the backsides of elephants gets old.

The New Realities

First, the future....

Come with us into the future. Into the vast darkness of the unknown. The time? The future. The place? It doesn't matter anymore. All borders have disappeared. Everything is available to everybody. It's a bright new world where distance and accessibility have been eliminated as "hindrances". It's all about utilitarianism and experience, along with a big hit of indulgence and affordability. The "middle of the road" is gone.

Come take a walk with us. Take a walk down Retail Road Future:

Everybody is selling. There was a time when supermarkets competed with supermarkets, and restaurants competed with restaurants. Not anymore, everyone is selling food.

The big box stores are nothing new but they are still growing, and the club stores are in the same position.

The growth of the opening price point/ private label stores, such as Aldi and Lidl, has shown there is a huge market for this format for all demographics.

Convenience stores are selling more food every year, as consumers demand more convenience- and tobacco use continues its decline. Dollar Stores that once sold variety items are selling more food every year, while adding coolers and freezers.

Pharmacies have gone way beyond selling drugs and related products. Many pharmacies have as many aisles of food as other non-food products. They are also adding coolers and freezers.

It's not just "stores" taking the business from the supermarkets. On-line shopping, such as Amazon is growing by leaps and bounds. And since Amazon has purchased Whole Foods, it is anyone's guess what they will do next with formats like Amazon Go.

There are many companies that sell that food, which we rarely consider. For example, when one thinks of HSN or QVC, they think jewelry, computers or clothing. But they sell food and lots of it. Just look at their website and you will see an assortment of food, from candy to turkeys and crabs! However, if you don't want to bother to place an order with the TV shopping channels, you can buy subscription services that will send you food every month; or, in some cases, every day if you desire.

For example, subscription services such as Graze or Paleo box, or Love with Food, will send you an assortment of food at any interval. If you want everything you need to prepare a full meal for yourself, count on Blue Apron or Hello Fresh or any other meal subscription service, to send you everything you need to make a meal for yourself or your family.

There are some formats to watch for in the future that are just now growing. Vending is going to be more than just candy and soda. Japan has shown us you can profitably sell all sorts of food in the multiple climate-controlled machines. Watch out for the building supply giants. They have contractors coming in all day to by materials, and it saves then a stop if they can pick up lunch or snacks.

Customer lifestyle is the differentiating factor by store. When everything costs the same, the connection must be deeper. So, all retailers picked a lifestyle and catered entirely to that lifestyle. Hunters? Of course, you have your camping equipment, easy-to-prepare food, shelf-stable goods, flash freezing equipment, apparel, and boats all under one roof.

Envision it as a Bass Pro Shop with a full assortment of the appropriate food and supplies. Couples with no families? A "no kid" zone of meals that can be prepared in 15 minutes, a store open 24 hours, an online offer that will deliver your goods within an hour anywhere you want it. Think of it as a pizza delivery for all goods, including clothing and accessories. Remember, formats have no borders. It's the lifestyle that matters. Retailers in the future satisfy every single need for a particular lifestyle. It's a connection that is almost unbreakable.

Accessibility of goods is seamless to the customer. They really don't care how you get it to them. They just want it. It's up to you to figure out the logistics. Remember, the stores that cater to all customers are gone by now. You own the lifestyle, you can anticipate demand, you are responsible for a seamless supply chain. Don't bother the customers with the details. As Nike says, "Just Do It."

Cheap and indulgent work together in this society. We want everything as cheap as possible, and love telling our friends about the deals. But, at the same time, we need the latest technological breakthrough gadget, we want decadent cakes, we want to be "first movers" on all new, trendy or "limited time only" items. Yes, it's tough as a retailer; but, it's all about the customer. It's about feeling smart. What should be cheap is cheap, but we all want to treat ourselves as well. Think of it this way: the ingredients should be affordable, and the result should taste like a million bucks.

There are no borders between digital, social, in-store or real life. The alternate worlds of online have blurred everything to the point where it's all one world. Today's world is like one big mixture of YouTube, Twitch, Twitter, Tik Tok, Instagram, and Snapchat . It's about being entertained, being part of a larger society across the globe, and about a borderless existence. As retailers, we had to understand how the next generation was being hard-wired to think of their world in terms of one steady flow of theatre, indulgence, and communication with hundreds at the same time. Experience is the king!

Everyone cares about everything. Yes, it was already brewing about ten years ago, when it became apparent that we could no longer ravage the earth for profits, we could no longer kill off our ozone and expect not to be fried by our own sun, we could no longer lay waste to the same vegetation that provided us with oxygen, we could no longer sit by idly while people were starving in Africa, we could no longer waste 20% of our food and think the planet could sustain a wasteful stewardship, that we could no longer keep eating pesticide-laden foods and expect to have long and healthy lives.

The desire for money was subdued by the need to "do good", to be part of the solution, to help Mother Earth survive and thrive for the next thousand years, to be part of one world, one people, one voice. You see, the amount of information flowing at light speed across the globe opened our eyes to the rest of the world, to the needs of the many, the plight of those we previously could ignore, the impact of non-sustainable farming on the soil, the impact of a civilization that was overly "consumerized".

It was an epiphany to an entire generation, and it stuck. The entire population started caring, wanted to only patronize those retailers who had a social conscience, started growing their own food. And it's not just a tagline....it is a real overt desire to be part of the solution, to be a contributor to the good of society. The retailers without a social conscience went out of business five years ago.

The future is not that far from now. In fact, the seeds are already planted and they are being watered vigorously. It's already happening. Formats are blurring, the middle ground is disappearing, customer lifestyle is in the driver's seat, having a social conscience is becoming table stakes. The seeds are sprouting everywhere. You might say the future is already here....

Start and End with the Customer

The perspective, and ostensibly the most important point of view you need: the customer is at the center of everything we do in Food Marketing. It's not the other way around- you don't create a format or offer and convince the customer to see you as a solution to their lives. It's their life, you get to be a part of it if they want you to be part of it. Having said that, there is plenty you can do to ensure you have a better chance than your competition. In this chapter, we will make connections between customer evolution, trends and power, and how that is changing the game- and what you can do about it.

Reality is….you might not make it. The customer has been "Amazon'd", they expect assortment from all over the world available at their fingertips, they'd like food delivered in an hour, and they expect full price transparency. If you cannot come to this realization, it's time to close this book, literally and figuratively. The customer wants to know "What makes you special?" If you cannot wake up every morning and know exactly what makes you special, then you probably aren't. It's okay, maybe the food industry isn't for you. It's a cutthroat, low margin, high turn business where every penny counts.

Understanding you're still reading, then let's make you special. Let's figure this customer out, and then maybe figure out how to "read the tea leaves" and stay ahead of changing trends.

The Generations

You hear so much about the changing of the generations! Baby Boomers to Millennials to Centennials. The "Silent" generation…. what a terrible thing to call someone. The thing to remember about generations, is it's just a start. You cannot "bucket" an entire generation into groups, and "market" to them. People are much too individualistic to be thrown into buckets. And, if you hear someone mention Millennials, make them stop! That cohort has grouped 15 years of people together and decided to treat them the same. Don't do it. Avoid bucketing, but *do* look for patterns. Here are a few:

The customers on the "up trend" in buying power have mostly never seen a life without the internet and a smartphone in their possession. In fact, the Centennials (Gen Z) claim over 95% smartphone ownership. It's not "different" to them to have all this power- they've never not had it. Using a phone for a shopping list, using it to look up health attributes of their food, using it to find hot deals, and using it to check your price versus the rest of the world- it's all second nature.

Multicultural is the norm. A striking fact about the changing of the United States population: 21% of those over 75 years old are non-white. 46% of the US 18-21 years old are non-white, including 22% identifying as Hispanic. It is expected 90% of the US population growth the next five years will be coming from non-white. Look at your team. Do you reflect the future?

Health and wellness is here to stay. It's a great trend, and hopefully lasts indefinitely. Looking up calories and ingredients on the smartphone is here and now. Full transparency about what you are putting in your products is crucial. And, if you manufacture goods and/or are a retailer with a strong private label offering, get those bad ingredients out! Why are you waiting to get the high fructose corn syrup out of your drink? You know it's not healthy, they know it's not healthy, so why leave bad ingredients in until the government tells you to take it out? Come on, think customer first!

Big spending is gone. The next generation of shoppers is showing they like multiple shopping trips. Whether it's because of money, or smaller family units, shopping is so much closer to the eating of that food today than at any time in the past! Shrink your store footprint, make it easy to navigate, trim your assortment to simplify decision making, and make sure your pack sizes are manageable. With the urbanization of the population, massive club packs and massive packs of meats are just not who we are. Let the customer know you appreciate their coming in four or five times a week.

Remove chokepoints. Checkout free is the future. It's a freight train with no brakes. It shouldn't have any either, the registers have always been the worst part of shopping from a customer point of view. Sorry, Polly running the register and holding conversations with each customer only made the next person in line angry. I love your conversation, but not at the expense of my time! If you are not able to offer checkout free yet, then go with self-checkout. Here's the mindset you need: self-checkout is actually offering **good** customer service. It's not a lamentable lack of personal interaction, it's getting the customers out of the chokepoint they hate. Look at Walmart, they switched to self-checkout, including using the belts, and do you see a line at Walmart anymore?

"Compare at" is rocking! If you shop TJ Maxx, you know "compare at". It's combining the customer desire to find "deals", to find discounted treasures, and it's giving the customer something to share with their friends. Everyone wants to say, "This is usually $28, and I stole it for $18!" Everyone. This is unabashedly how retail will work going forward- you have got to make the customer look smart to themselves and their friends. Nothing is smarter than getting a good deal. It doesn't matter how much money you have.

Limited Time Only is right there with "compare at". Same type of idea, except this one adds scarcity. Now, instead of getting a discount, the customer will pay a premium just because they also want to share with their friends they got something no one else got. Scarcity works! Tell someone there is a "limit of 6", and they'll buy 6. LTO never fails to awaken the competitive spirit in customers.

Resale is coming to the forefront. It's a sharing economy of Air BnB and Uber and renting jewelry, so it only makes sense resale is on a tear! Go in Plato's Closet, or Goodwill or ThredUp, or even the resale pop ups appearing in Macy's and JC Penney, and it's a trend for next five years at least. Bargain hunting in secondhand clothes is not for those who "need" it anymore, it's for those who want to tell their friends what they found.

Everything is shared. Yes, these trends are all running together. Everything is shared. Great bargains, super finds, LTO's, in-store events….they are immediately shared with friends.

Be social. This is where generations are splitting a bit. Facebook isn't cool, but it exists. It's not dead. Instagram is removing likes, so I'm not sure about the future of Instagram. People live for "likes". Snapchat and its filters skew towards a younger generation. And you may want to learn about twitch, if you don't know about it yet. Twitch isn't an uncontrollable muscle spasm anymore, it's a place to watch people game. Yup, and it's hot!

Diets are changing. Vegetarian is huge (around $300B in sales) and growing, pescetarian (no meat, but will eat fish) is not far behind, plant based and vegan are trending as well. Diets have changed based upon health benefits (or harm from what is being avoided) and/or climate and world impacts. The red meat methane issue has been discussed for years, but has gained steam.

The environment and social consciousness are top of mind. Yes, these trends tend to piggyback (cowback?) each other. The concern for the environment has escalated, as well as the social consciousness of how you treat your employees, how you treat your suppliers, how you treat people in general- it's all bubbled to the top.

Tell your story. You cannot operate without a story. Just don't do it. You are special for some reason. Tell people about it. Why should they care about you, your products, your store? People want to know you are not a monolithic generic massive corporation. You are run by people and you have a story. Integrate that story into everything you do, and all marketing messages.

Guns, drugs, cannabis, and race. Sounds like a bad joke, doesn't it? The point is, trends and social shifts are happening constantly. You, as a retailer or consumer goods company, need to understand how you fit into the narrative. Gun control and freedom to carry weapons seems like an endless debate in this country. You should have a stance. I'm not going to tell you what it should be. These are emotional debates, with less facts and more rhetoric being spewed by all "sides". The truth is you cannot stand on the sideline. Take a stance. The public will either like it or not. Being neutral is not an option.

Virtual reality and augmented reality. A trend shift towards gaming and virtual reality is afoot. If you play in that arena, you should embrace the trend. Where a retailer could see major gains, though, is augmented reality; where you take reality and change it in some way. Show the customer how the shirt would fit them, how the product would look in their pantry, how the meal could come together from your ingredients. You can do this right now. I would say, a virtual reality shopping experience of walking your store and placing things in a shopping basket would be pretty cool!

Living alone and unmarried. No, that's not an ad for alcohol, it's reality. People are either waiting to get married, or do not see the point. And divorce rate is at record levels. A single mom or dad, or a person living alone, has a massive shift in their expectations of you versus those with large families. Large families are not the trend. And, included in here is the "sharing economy", or the desire to not own assets, but to rent them or "borrow" (using an Uber is borrowing an asset) them. How that fits into your retail should be part of your strategic discussions.

Robots and drones. The trend to either offer kiosks to replace order taking or drones to deliver products has gone from "way out there" bizarre to "hey, that would work". A world of drones dropping off our morning coffee is not far off.

Workforce participation and expectation. The generation coming into the most buying power has seen their parents "work until you die", they've seen people lose their minds over the stock market, they've seen illnesses and diseases because of overwork- and they don't want that. Do not interpret what we are saying as the next generation is lazy. Too many people brand the "next generation" as lazy. It's not that at all. There is always a Bell Curve of over-achieving, being good enough, and being lazy- no matter your generation. That's called being human. The "work till you die" outlook has been replaced with "I want to enjoy and like my life, and make enough money to live well." Enjoying life's experiences isn't being saved for two vacations a year.

Malls are dead. Their death was predicted for years, and it's here. Don't misunderstand mall "traffic" with mall "success". There are people in malls, but they're not buying anything. In fact, malls have kind of become a nice place to walk around when it's too hot or too cold out, and you just want to walk around. Other than those who have not adopted the health and wellness trend, very few people are eating there, very few people are buying anything, and the comedy clubs and bowling alleys and laser tag places are not working. If you are establishing retail locations, best suggestion is to avoid the mall- the customers are.

Store brands are cool. Studies show the majority of the population has become so brand non-loyal, they don't care about buying brands. And, if you're in craft beer, you know this- sometimes an established brand is a negative. Store brands are cool, they provide a value, they provide margin rates for retailers, and they encourage store loyalty. Store brands are a winner, and should be cultivated. As you will read later in this book, they can even give promotional retailers a sound base of value offerings for their customers.

Inflation is the only growth you should expect. What I mean by this is do not set your annual budgets to *show growth*. Set your plans to *achieve* growth. Consumer goods grew at 2% last year, but units did not grow. That's called inflation. If you budget inflation, and let all costs increase to that budget, you're stuck raising prices if you cannot achieve unit growth. Go for unit growth. And, make sure all operating statements show both sales and units. If you show sales growth only, and are not increasing tonnage, you are putting yourself out of business. If you are just learning Food Marketing, read this one again. Units drive future success. Inflation falsely covers retailer issues. You must measure units and tonnage! To add one more piece to it, measure sales, units and tonnage as "same store". In other words, year over year, what existed last year versus same this year. It's the best measure of true health of any product or store.

Wealth gaps are real. This is not a shift in the population. Wealth gaps have always existed. They are possibly more pronounced today, or at least more visible. It's a real issue. A company that shows it knows its customer will be viewed as a company that cares about its customer. We're not saying "give everything back", you need profitability to run a company. We are saying, though, care about your customer. If you are seen as helping provide solutions to society's issues, you integrate into your customers' lives. That's a good thing.

Data works. You have point of sale data, you have loyalty card data, you have tons of data. Past purchase behavior tends to predict future behavior. Overlapping purchases by similar groups tends to predict purchase behavior by other similar customers. You *can* be part of the solution for constant refilling (auto-replenish) of commodity items, suggestions for other purchases, making lives easier. For some reason, it seems only Amazon understands this- and Dunnhumby. Using data to predict future behavior makes analytical workers in the future highly valuable.

Cities are the future. Or, adding to that, "smart" cities are the future. Ask a teenager today if they like driving. Interestingly, driving is not important anymore. Kids in the 80's, and before that, were all about getting licenses and getting the "freedom". Today, a city where things can be delivered to you, where you can walk or take public transportation, where all your solutions are within a mile or two- yeah, it's pretty interesting to the next generation coming up in buying power. Translated: have an urban footprint and plan for your stores, and an urban size plan for your products. Offer delivery or "click and collect". It won't be taken up by everybody, but you still need to offer it. Urbanization is a strong trend!

Retailers with expertise sharing space is the future. Target combining with CVS was just the beginning. Kroger and Walgreens, etc. Rather than develop expertise, why not let experts offer that service for your aggregated customers? Think, if you could find a Lidl or Aldi inside a Target? Game changer, right?

Mobile everything. Whatever you offer and whatever you do, it should be seamlessly available on a mobile device. An easy mobile interaction! Not constantly looking for passwords (make them use thumbprint), not constantly asking for credit card information....make it as seamless as walking the store. Seamless mobile is here now, and is a customer expectation.

Winners won't always win and losers won't always lose.
Sears was on top of the world, until it wasn't. A&P ruled from
coast to coast, until it didn't. TJ Maxx was a bit player, until
it came into its own. Walmart was suffering until it grabbed a
toehold, and is kicking butt again! Aldi was slowly expanding
until Lidl came to the US. Target was cool, then wasn't, and
now is....they have found their mojo again!

Winning means taking it from somebody. I apologize for the
cold hard truth, but winning means someone will probably lose.
The beauty of capitalism! Market share is a zero-sum game.
Have the killer mentality and you're going to be a winner!

The Imperceptible Change

These new realities are not easy to see. You go in your store
every day, and things look about the same. It's like going into
a garden and trying to watch a rose open. You'll watch and
watch. Nothing happens. But, in a day or two, there it is --
full in bloom and beginning to fade.

That's like watching change take place in the supermarket
business. Change is often hard to see. But, it's happening!

When we were in Germany, we asked a group of supermarket
managers, "Could you tell us how the `typical German' eats?"

One answered, "Ja, I can tell you." And so, he described how
the mother -- who was a housewife -- would cook dinner for
the family. And about 6:00 in the evening the husband, wife,
and children would sit down to a family dinner.

We asked him, "Is that the way your family ate last night?" He
said "Nein. But my family is slightly different than the typical
German family."

There were five others in the room. We asked another person,
"Is that the way you ate last night?" "Nein. My family didn't eat
that way either last night."

Then we asked the others. Of the entire group, not a single
person's family ate the way the "typical German family" eats.

30

About this time a young woman came into the room with coffee. We asked one of the managers to ask her how her family ate last night. Guess what? Her family didn't eat the way a typical German family eats. But, as she explained, her family wasn't the "typical German family."

Finally, when we were leaving the store, we asked a manager to ask a young lady who was sitting at the information desk. Her description of how her family ate was identical to how the "typical German family" eats. And what do you think those managers said to us? "Ja! Ja! You see what we mean. It's exactly the way the Germans eat."

What would we tell Germans about the typical family in the United States? Would we describe it as a husband at work, a wife at home with one or more children? If we defined it that way in the past, we would have been right. That would have classified approximately 50 percent of the households in the United States. And those who were atypical aspired to be like that other 50 percent.

Sometimes the family changes are more obvious. The vision of the Norman Rockwell family is now replaced by the Modern Family in the popular TV show.

But today, less than 15 percent of the United States households consists of husbands at work and wives at home with one or more children. The largest household type in the US today is single person households.

Today Is Different. And It's Becoming More So Every Day.

Four driving forces are leading to the change.

Driving Force #1: *More Splintered Markets*

The Gen X and Millennials are getting a lot of media attention. But, within those markets, there are still big differences. Whether they are Gen Z or Millennials, Gen X or even the Silent Generation, the typical United States family isn't dad at work, mom at home, kids at school, what does the typical family look like? In fact, do we even have married families anymore?

There no longer is a typical American family. America now consists of a mosaic of households. In the past few years, many terms have emerged to describe this diversity. For example:

Latchkey Kids: Kids who come home while both
          parents are at work.

Sincoms: Single incomes with outrageous mortgages.

POSSJQ: Persons of opposite sex sharing living quarters.

Aging Yuppies: Aging young urban professionals

TOBY: Too old to be a yuppie.

Baby Boomers: An increasingly older portion of the population.
          The last of the "greed is good" cohort.

Millennials: Too large a group to lump into one bucket, but
          reflective of a group that saw their parents go back to
          work when the economy contracted. Some are in mid-
          career, and some are recently out of college.

Centennials: Tech innate, never had a life without five devices
          around them telling them everything immediately,
          checking prices on handhelds, ordering products
          seamlessly through any platform, and much more
          concerned about social consciousness, the
          environment, and experiencing life.

Skippies: School kids with income and purchasing power.

Sandwichers: Adults who care for both their children and aging
          parents.
Opals: Older people with active lifestyles.

Again, note that these are new terms characterizing our newly splintered, distracted market place. And some of these terms describe lifestyles which just a few years ago would not have been heard of in our society.

Any way you look at it, the USA market is increasingly bucketed into small homogeneous groups. Obviously, these differing segments have different needs.

But these differing needs would not be so significant to supermarkets if it were not for three other driving forces. Let's look at them.

Driving Force #2: *Flexible Manufacturing (sometimes called Lean Production)*

We now have the technology to produce a wide variety of products at little extra cost. For example, Campbell Soup Company used to have trucks filled with tomatoes lined up outside their factories, from August to September. That's when they made tomato soup. They would make one batch a year. Today their soup production lines run an average of only four hours. And they do it economically. The ability for companies to produce tailored inventory closer to consumption time is an impactful change in inventory flow.

Driving Force #3: *I Can Get it to You Yesterday*

We've become much more proficient in logistics. Just-in-time inventory, continuous replenishment, cross docking, and other facets of ECR make shipments of small quantities feasible. Add the fact you can find anything you want online, and receive it potentially within hours, and everything is different about how consumers procure their goods.

Driving Force #4: *Massive Change in Media*

This force has had, arguably, one of the biggest impacts on modern marketing. The range of communication media has tripled in size, as all sorts of social media has changed the landscape. Consumers are trading off TV watching to cell phone ubiquity. You have people using YouTube as their primary media channel, communicating with hundreds of people constantly through Facebook, Snapchat, Instagram, Tik Tok, Twitter, etc. Finding people and communicating with them about your brand is increasingly difficult. You need to find them in their "opt in" groups, where they gather with similar people. It may be family and friends, or it may be just people with similar interests. Either way, they are talking. Your job is to get in there and join the conversation.

So, now our markets are splintered and these "splinters" have differing needs. Of great importance is that today we have the ability to satisfy these diverse markets. We can now produce and ship, economically, a wide variety of products to these splintered markets. And we have the technology to communicate to these splintered markets. The key is embracing the bifurcation and distraction. Embrace it. That's our present and future.

These four driving forces point out there are no longer markets for products that everybody likes a little, there are only markets for products that somebody likes a lot.

And, it follows that there is no longer demand for supermarkets that everybody likes a little. There is only demand for supermarkets that somebody likes a lot.

Today's Change Is a Double-Edged Sword

One Edge: A Threat

Trying to recapture the old ways of doing business just won't work: It would be violating the Law of the Hole which states: "When you're in a hole, Stop Digging!"

More of the same is just going to get supermarkets into a deeper hole. Time is running out.

We may not see that change taking place. But it is. Those who don't look at this change as an opportunity won't be looking very long.

The Other Edge: An Opportunity

When change is taking place there's great opportunity because most people will not recognize the change. Or if they do, they won't act on it.

The next three steps show you how you can capitalize on the new world of supermarkets, by making people feel like your supermarket is their supermarket.

STEP 2: BE LOYAL TO YOUR CUSTOMERS

Coca-Cola's Retailing Research Council came up with this major finding: Basically customers are not as loyal to supermarkets as previously thought.

To wit, the average customer was visiting a given supermarket only about once every two weeks. Now, this is significant given the average customer visits a supermarket 2.2 times each week. Coca-Cola's study also found that customers had a yearly defection rate of 25 percent to 50 percent.

Crazy!

And part of this customer disloyalty is caused by a distorted view of the way supermarkets usually view loyalty.

Loyalty: A Measure of The Supermarkets' Relationships to Their Customers. Not A Measure of Customers Relationships' to Supermarkets.

We're accustomed to thinking about loyalty in terms of something that people are to us. Specifically, we think of loyalty as a measure of the strength of customers' relationships to our supermarket.

Loyalty shouldn't be considered as a measure of customers' relationships to us. Loyalty should be considered as a measure of our relationship to customers.

Does it seem like we're parsing words?

Well, we're not.

If you are loyal to your customers by doing the kinds of things that delight them and do those things better than your competitors, then your customers will come back, time after time, to your supermarket.

So, instead of trying to figure out how to make customers more loyal to you, decide how you can be more loyal to your customers.

So, how, specifically, can you be loyal to your customers?

Historically supermarkets relied on location and low price. Basically, they were all the same and had the same products. Thus, if you could be physically closer to customers, and/or sell it cheaper, you would win the profit game.

But, not anymore. There are so many new players and new supermarket formats that offering exactly what consumers want will, or can, beat out price or location. One of the most successful supermarket chains is Wegman's. They are certainly not the cheapest. The old algorithm of the primary shopper being a mile or so from the store was changed by Walmart and Costco, where consumers will drive 25 miles to shop there.

Many supermarkets believe they can buy loyalty with low prices. Well, sometimes price may conquer all. Some people will go to the store that offers the lowest price. Some people will go from store to store cherry picking the specials.

But not everyone.

Two examples. First, a young professional. Both he and his spouse work. They have one daughter, age six. The two parents are always seeking quality time with their daughter (Note that research reveals that taking children to supermarkets is a major drawback and source of stress to the shopper.).

He does most of the family grocery shopping and always goes to a certain supermarket. Why? Because the supermarket has a playroom and his daughter loves to go there while he's doing the shopping.

Is the supermarket the lowest price supermarket in town? He didn't know. As he explained, "I have so little time to spend with my daughter. I do the grocery shopping and she goes with me to the supermarket. The trip to, and returning from, the supermarket is a real enjoyment for both of us. She's either excited about going to the supermarket's playroom or explaining, with delight, what happened at the supermarket. That makes the trip enjoyable for me."

Would he go to the supermarket if its prices were five percent higher than other supermarkets?

"Sure." How about ten percent? A pause. Then, "Perhaps."

The second example: An elderly widow in her mid-eighties. She lives by herself. She has trouble doing her shopping because she no longer drives.

She always goes to one supermarket because the supermarket has a van that takes her to the store. After she does her shopping, the van takes her home.

Is the supermarket the lowest price supermarket in town? She said, "I don't think so. But it's so convenient to shop at this supermarket. Besides, there are some regulars who always ride the van. It's almost like a club."

These are only two examples. But as you can imagine, there's countless more.

Small wonder that so many shopper loyalty programs have failed. Getting a few cents off -- even in a convenient manner -- is just not that important to a number of market segments.

And one more point on price, you can always be beat on price. A retailer with deeper pockets, a retailer trying to establish themselves in the marketplace, an operator with less services than you offer. All of them can beat you on price. Price is not a differentiator.

Make Your Supermarket's Philosophy Be: "Satisfying Your Customer in a Most Delightful Way and Profits Will Be Your Reward."

Solve your customers' problems - week after week- and they'll want to come to your store <u>trip</u> after <u>trip</u>. Having the lowest price isn't always necessary -- or sufficient.

We know this begs a question, "What do customers really want?" And you're probably also saying, "You can't satisfy everyone." Well, we're glad you asked. Keep reading!

STEP 3: SELECT YOUR TARGET MARKETS

You can't satisfy everyone.

That's right. You can't. It's a salad bowl out there. Not a melting pot. Try to be the dressing on the parts of the salad you know you can delight.

There are Two Ways to Cook an Elephant

Suppose you've got an elephant to cook (we seem to mention elephants a lot, don't we?). There are two ways you can do it. One way is to find a pot big enough to hold the elephant. But, right off you have a problem. Have you ever seen a pot that big?

Fortunately, there's a second way. Cut the elephant up, and cook it in small pots. Your task is now manageable. And, you still get to eat the whole elephant. We must add: the above was metaphorical, and we do not espouse the cooking of elephants.

Cutting up the Market

Following the same principle, how can you cut up markets so you don't have the impossible task of trying to find a large enough pot -- supermarket -- for everyone?

To make customers feel like your supermarket is their supermarket, you've got to decide who you are going to delight. You can't satisfy everybody. You're going to leave too much on the table for some and not enough on the table for others.

Let's look at some possible slices -- segments -- that could be specifically served: families with children, teenagers, college students, singles, elderly, upscale, inner city, Hispanic, African Americans, Asians, health conscious.

It may be that, for a given supermarket, you can target more than one segment. For example, there's no reason why you can't serve the singles segment, and also have a section of your supermarket for the health conscious. Or, cater to the upscale and have a special part of your store for upscale Jewish patrons.

Keep in mind that if you are targeting a specific market, you don't restrict people of any group or segment from shopping in your store. You won't be asking for ID to get in. Maybe the best example is McDonalds. They target kids; and they do everything to make their stores perfect for kids, from kid's meals, playgrounds and a spokesclown. However, anyone can go in and buy whatever they want. Targeting doesn't mean some people aren't welcome. It means, for some people, this is the very best choice.

We're not talking about firing some of your present customers who don't happen to fit into the niche or niches you're targeting. No, you aren't going to refuse their business. But you're going to put your dollars where they'll give you the biggest bang -- serving selected target markets. The key is to understand who you really want to target.

Targeting Markets Requires Proactive Thinking

To make people feel like your supermarket is their supermarket, select the target market (or markets) you can best serve, and want to serve. Then make sure you satisfy these customers, and in a most delightful way (not just marginally satisfying them).

We know you may be thinking, "Isn't that what category management is all about? Isn't category management adjusting product assortments to the customers that are coming into the store?"

Absolutely, yes. And absolutely a right step in the right direction.

But we're talking about something different than that. We're talking about getting the kind of people you want into your store in the first place, not changing the assortment to who is in the store.

In other words, it's not reacting to who is in the store, but it's proactively deciding who you want in the store. Once you decide who you want to target, then it's making that target market feel as if your store is their store.

For example, if you are targeting Foodies, you may have more exotic vegetables such as small bok choi or fresh bean sprouts (along with the usual products); but, if are targeting the price sensitive, you would have a totally different assortment and no bok choi.

Operational Suggestions

Let's look at some operational suggestions for selecting your target markets.

Decide Which Segment You Are Going to Delight
At the corporate level, decide which markets you are going to delight. Answer these questions:

What kinds of segments are you now serving?
What kinds of segments are in your trading area?
What kinds of segments do your management, and other employees, feel comfortable serving?
What kinds of segments could you best serve, that is, what kinds of segments could you satisfy, in a most delightful way, while reaching your sales and profit objectives?

Appoint Target Market Managers

It will take savvy to carry out successful target marketing programs. It's not the best policy to leave developing these programs to amateurs. Or to store managers who are probably overworked -- or who may not have the experience. And one tip, an intelligent person can learn target markets, but an intelligent person who actually is part of that market? Gold!

One supermarket, with about 100 stores, created a Hispanic marketing director. She was responsible for implementing programs targeted to the Hispanic market. Unfortunately, she did not have the necessary authority to deal with store managers. Some store managers objected to the Hispanic programs; and others, with a small Hispanic population, wanted it. If you take this suggestion, make sure the appointed target market manager has the authority needed to accomplish their task.

Decide Which Stores Can Best Delight Various Segments

Which markets you target may vary from store to store. It depends, mainly, upon present customers and the type of people who live in the store's trading area.

A store may serve multiple market segments. Again, this depends on its present customers, and who's in the store's trading area.

Services to Help Determine Target Markets

It used to be expensive to get information about the people in your trading area. Now, we're fortunate. We can get excellent data at a very reasonable cost. You have your own loyalty card data, you have services who will mine your data for you, etc. Studies have shown pinpointed communication returns 9:1 sales to dollars spent. Weekly ads? 3:1

Nielsen sells a system called Spectra. This has just about everything you could possibly want to know about the population around a store, as well as the extent to which competitors target those consumers. Now this might be a little expensive, if you fail to get a supplier to help pay for it. Use nearby university students to comb through the US statistical data, to get demographics around the store. They are usually cheap and good researchers.

"You Can't Be All Things to All People." So Easy To Say, Yet So Difficult to Put into Practice.
Suppose you've selected the target markets you want to serve. To be loyal to these target markets -- to delight them better than competition -- is going to require 110 percent of your efforts. And, for some programs, additional monies.

For example, suppose you decide to target families with young children. You may decide that you'll need easily accessible rest rooms with changing tables and a playroom. This will reduce your selling space and increase your operating costs (somebody must keep the rest rooms clean and supervise the playroom).

This means you'll have to neglect some segments. For instance, if your target market's needs demand a number of amenities, you'll probably not be able to cater to those who want more depth and breadth of merchandise and/or the lowest possible prices. You hope they will still come to your supermarket. But, you can't try to delight them. Some segments just want different things and are unwilling to pay for certain amenities that delight other segments.

To say "You can't be all things to all people" is easy to say. Yet it is so difficult to put into practice.

For example, one supermarket executive claimed he firmly believed in targeting. He acknowledged that if you want families with children to come to your store, shopping trip after shopping trip, there were certain things that the supermarket had to do -- to offer -- to delight this segment. And so on.

At the close of our conversation he asked, "Have you been to our new store?"

We said that we hadn't. "Oh, you ought to go there. It's really our best store."

And then we asked, "If we were to walk through that store, if we were to talk to your employees, would we know who you were targeting?"
"Hey! We're trying to get everybody to come to our store."

He didn't believe -- or really understand targeting. He was just intellectualizing.

A postscript. We visited this store. Breadth and depth of assortments. Wide aisles. Clean. And advertised low prices.

But, for one of the major segments he claimed they were targeting (parents with children), there weren't easily accessible restrooms with changing tables. Or a playroom. And so on. The store was just another new store for everyone. But it was a store that didn't delight anyone. The middle of the road is where you find roadkill.

One last comment on targeting. When we were on a supermarket visitation trip for some European guests, we visited one store and we asked "who is the target audience.?' The store's manager was very articulate and clearly understood who they were trying to delight. Shortly after that we visited another store and asked the same questions. The store manager asked, "what do you mean." I responded, "who is your target customer. He responded, "are you crazy, we want everybody." I don't want to give the name of that store, but its initials are A&P.

STEP 4: FIND OUT YOUR TARGET MARKET(S) SHOPPING PROBLEMS- SOLVE THEM

Given you now know the kinds of target markets you can best serve, how can you be loyal to them? How can you solve their problems?

Category Management is Necessary, But Not Always Enough.

It usually will take more than product assortments. For example, why do people go to McDonald's? For good old fatty, high cholesterol junk food at reasonable prices? Not likely.

Aren't there cheaper hamburgers at other places? Aren't there better hamburgers at other places? Of course.

There are other things about McDonald's that make it attractive to some people. For example, one of the segments that McDonald's targets is kids. So McDonald's has, for starters, playgrounds, a spokesclown: Ronald McDonald, coloring books, clean bathrooms, kids meals, kids promotions and free birthday parties.

These non-product amenities are a major reason why McDonald's is so successful and such a tough competitor. Just having the right menu is often not sufficient.

Now, don't get us wrong. We believe that product assortment is very, very important. And clearly the progress that supermarkets have made in category management is very significant. But, category management by itself is usually not sufficient. Category Management will keep you profitable and effective in your assortment, a total delight environment complements the offer. Remember, it also works in reverse: if the playgrounds and restrooms were perfect, but there was no food, they'd become a pretty easy competitor quite quickly.

Solving Your Target Market(s) Problems with Product assortment

When choosing a target market, it becomes imperative that you consider a shopping basket, and not just a single product or product category. Equally important is that all the category managers are on the same page. In one example, a category manager realized she was not selling much mango baby food. In fact, the peas etc. we're selling about 10 to 1 better. So, like any "old time" manager, she took the slow selling mango off the shelf and replaced it with a high velocity variety. Within a few weeks, all baby food sales had a slight decline. Shortly after that, the other categories, such as the baby diapers, baby formula et al had decreased. Of course, those managers were shocked, as they had done nothing differently. Of course, mothers that want the one jar of mango, but who also bought the ten jars of peas, left for another store that still had mango. We can't say it enough, it's about the customer.

Good example (handwritten margin note)

Solving Your Target Market(s) Problems with Non-Product Amenities

Every supermarket offers some non-product amenities. Still, our research shows it's in this area (in contrast with category management) that most supermarkets are much further behind in their targeting efforts. For this reason, let's use an example on ways -- other than product assortment -- that could make people feel like your supermarket is their supermarket.

An Example: Elderly

Suppose you're targeting the elderly. What are some of the shopping problems they have? For one, they tire quickly. Solution: Give them places to sit down. A typical response to this solution is, "Now wait a minute. We could put shippers in those places. We could make another X number of dollars." But, if you want to delight older Americans so they'll come to your store trip after trip, then having places for them to sit down is what you'll have to have.

Another problem. Sometimes the elderly need more assistance. Solution: train your staff so they'll be sensitive to the elderly's needs and know how to help them. For example, if they see older persons struggling to get large containers off the shelf, they'll recognize that it's embarrassing for the elderly to ask for help and will go up and ask, "Can I assist you with this?" And, for heaven's sake, make the restrooms accessible- and maybe even in the back, as well as front, of the store!

Operational Suggestions

Develop A Plan for Each Market Segment You Want to Target

In Step 3, you decided which market segments you were going to target. At the corporate level, now develop a plan for each of these segments.

Your task is to put together programs that not only will delight your target market, but also be cost effective. It will take keen understanding of the target market to develop such marketing plans.

Clearly no role for amateurs. That's why, in Step 3, we recommended that you have target market managers.

Decide Which Stores Get Which Plan(s)
Every store probably won't be, and probably shouldn't be, targeting the same segments. So again, at the corporate level, decide which stores get which plans.

Modify Plan(s) According to the Unique Situations of Each Store

Although you've developed a plan for each segment, don't use these plans like you would cookie cutters. You may have developed, for instance, a plan for the teenage segment. Included in this plan was sponsoring a midsummer-night teenage dance in the stores' parking lots. However, such a dance might not be advisable for all the stores targeting teenagers.

Modify the plans for individual stores' unique market characteristics.

Let Your Strategy Dictate Your Tactics

The examples, given above, for solving target market problems seem logical and doable. Right?

Still they cost money, take up space, and/or require staff time to implement. And here's where many supermarkets draw the line. And here's where their targeting efforts, for all practical purposes, turn into sheer lip service.

If, for example, you want to target families with children, you've got to be loyal to them. You've got to solve their problems. And this will require expenditures.

We asked one supermarket executive, "Since families with children is one of your target markets, would you consider having a clown in the store on, say, Monday and Tuesday mornings?"

"Of course I would."

However, he went on to say, "But only if you could prove to me that every time a clown is in the store, we'd have enough sales increase to pay for the clown."
He missed the whole point (incidentally although this store was "targeting" families with children, it didn't have conveniently located rest rooms with changing tables, kids' clubs, kids' playrooms. And so on).

Do you think that McDonald's policy is: Only send Ronald McDonald to those places where, on the day Ronald is there, we're going to increase sales enough to pay for the visit?

Of course not!

Some amenities -- and product assortments -- although they might not be "cost effective," are necessary to help you to be loyal to your customers. Perhaps having a clown on the premises just might make supermarket shopping enjoyable to the kids (Or....scarier! Poor clowns, they tend to be designated as scary these days). This, in turn, might transform a chore to quality time, and a delight to the parents.

The clown might not increase your daily sales. Yet the presence of the clown might make these families with children return to your store, trip after trip, even though your store does not have the lowest prices. It just might help them feel like your supermarket is their supermarket.

Another example. We were visiting a supermarket that was serving the upscale. The owner pointed out to us six kinds of peppers and mentioned that the only kinds he sold in any quantities were the green and red. He hardly sold any of the other kinds. He said, "You know, I've got a bunch of products like these slow-moving peppers. Although these products have high margins, they cost me money because of their low turnover. So, why do I carry them? My customers expect to see products like this in a store like mine." He viewed these costs as necessary costs to be loyal to his customers.

Of course, you must guard against adding a host of product assortments and/or programs that do not enable you to make a profit. But you also must take care that you are loyal to your target market(s).

Let your strategy dictate your tactics

Overcoming Concerns

If there were no concerns about using target marketing, it would be <u>Standard Operating Procedure</u>. And, of course, it is not.

Many of the supermarket managers we talked with had reservations about a targeted approach. While most agreed it sounded good in theory, they voiced concerns about several implementation issues.

Their worries seemed to hinge on four potential problems areas: loss of chain image, loss of economies of scale, loss of management control, and not enough trained personnel to serve targeted markets.

These issues certainly appear to be potential issues, and deserve special attention. But, these problem areas can be solved if addressed from the point of view of "How can we make a targeted approach work," rather than, "How will targeting fit into the status quo of our operation?"

We looked at some supermarkets to see how they solved these problems. And, we talked with executives specifically about these problem areas. Here's what we found out.

Many supermarkets strive to promote a corporate identity, such as low prices, high quality meats and produce, wide selections, and/or fast check-out lanes. Then, they make sure that each store within the chain conforms to this image.

But within a chain, targeting different segments by different stores can muddle this image. Suppose for a given chain, that some of its stores are targeting only the elderly, some only families with children, some only upscale, some only Hispanics and some only inner city. What would happen when a customer who was accustomed to going to one of the chain's stores that targets the upscale goes to another one of the chain's stores that targets the inner city? This customer's reaction might be, "It's certainly not my supermarket," and perhaps they would shift their patronage to a different chain.

Some supermarket managers told us that, "The bark is much worse that the bite." In fact, the problem is more likely to be with chain management and not with store customers. Often corporate managers go from store to store asking the question, "Why doesn't this store do things the way other stores do? Let's simplify things by having uniformity." The "bark" may be a red herring created by management.

There's usually relatively little customer crossover from one chain's store to another of its stores. Even when this happens, a customer recognizes that this other store is targeting different customers and will continue to shop at "his/her" store.

To entirely avoid mixed images, a chain could take the ultimate step and give stores that serve different segments different names. Like Kroger or Loblaw's or even Publix and HEB. They differentiate the uniqueness of certain stores by changing the names of the stores. Sometimes where you cannot even tell it's part of the chain, and sometimes coupling the parent company name with the segmented store name.

Where the Rubber Meets the Road

Suppose you're targeting parents with children. And you have tactical programs in place to implement this strategy, such as: newborn promotions, home delivery, conveniently located bathrooms with changing tables, kid's clubs, etc.

The store personnel must make it work all day and every day. Low wages and high turnover suggest that store personnel may not be up to the task. Maybe so, but there are some steps you can take to help make employees more effective in carrying out your targeting problem.

First, keep targeting programs simple so they can be easily understood by all.

Next, assign specific people the responsibility for implementation. If it is everyone's responsibility, then invariably it winds up being no one's responsibility. Of course, everyone will be involved in carrying out the targeting programs.

Then, make sure that all store employees understand the store's strategy. Let's take a page from Walmart to see why this is important. We were recently on a Walmart superstore tour. But before we could go through the store, a manager spent over 30 minutes with our group explaining the store's strategy. He pointed out, "What you see in the store can only make sense in the context of what we are trying to accomplish - our strategy." This same type of briefing is necessary for employees if they are going to be effective in implementing your targeting programs.

Finally, be sure that all store employees are trained on how to delight target segments. It might not help you to increase employee retention, but it will help you to increase customer retention.

Cheaper by the Dozen

The third major concern was losses of economies of scale in such areas as purchasing, logistics, and promotion.

No doubt you save by buying for all stores. The process is simple: one plan-o-gram, one order form, fewer personnel, and more leverage with manufacturers. You don't have to bother with special items for only a few stores in your chain, so logistics are simpler. And just think, only one advertising campaign for your entire chain!

So, if different stores in your chain target different market segments, no doubt you will lose "efficiencies" in purchasing, logistics, and promotions; as well as in a host of other functional areas such as store design, construction and employee training. But, these losses are not necessarily killer factors.

For example, even in a targeted store environment, possibly 70 percent or more of the SKUs will be the same. This 70 percent will still retain most of the efficiencies of scale in purchasing and logistics.

Only a small subset of items will vary. For these products, you can get store delivery. In the new environment of partnership, manufacturers of specialty items will gladly work with you to help delight your targeted customers. After all, they are the manufacturers' target markets too.

With careful management, losses in efficiency can more than be made up for in gains in customer satisfaction, customer retention, and ultimately, in profits. And the objective of business is not to cut costs, but to make a profit.

Marketing Operates in a Fishbowl

Suppose at a store you have been targeting two segments: families with children and the elderly. You now decide that you are going to target solely families with children. So, you rearrange your product assortment and services to cater to that segment, families with children.

Elderly customers will be quick to notice now your store doesn't seem to be nearly as much like their store:

You no longer carry the products they are used to buying.

There's now a playroom for kids. But where are the benches to sit down?

And so, they complain.

How will top management react? Will they insist that the store go back to carrying products and services that please the elderly? Will it penalize store management for having dissatisfied customers?

Be sure that new criteria are used to judge store management. If you ask them to delight a specific target market, don't hold them accountable for pleasing everybody.

Then, there's the possibility of glitches in marketing programs. For example, let's suppose you have a special event for parents with children. Key to the special event is a coveted premium. You greatly underestimate demand. And to further complicate matters, your supplier cannot deliver additional premiums.

When things go wrong with marketing programs, everybody is aware of the slips. It can create bad publicity for the supermarket, as well as put jobs in jeopardy.

The more segments you target, the greater the possibility for snafus. You will have more programs and you will have less experienced personnel in charge of these programs.

There are two solutions to this problem. First, start out by targeting just one segment. Develop expertise before you start another. Second, develop modules for different segments at the corporate level. Make them idiot proof. Then corporate management should help store management decide which modules should be used at a given store.

A Final Word

These recommendations will help you resolve some of the problems inherent in tilting toward a more targeted strategy. The recommendations presented here are far from comprehensive: complete books could be written on each of the concerns. So, view these explanations as guidelines or starting points.

If, on the other hand, the specifics of your problems make them seem unique, keep this in mind. The guidelines presented here all resulted from problems that once seemed unique.

Target marketing is still evolving and nobody said it was easy. But, if other supermarkets can resolve their problems and make target marketing work, then so can you.

The Singles Target Market

Tactic Number: 1 **Bulk Up**

Tactic: Offer all produce in bulk (not prepackaged). Also, offer half, quarters, or even sliced melons, heads of lettuce, pineapples, coconuts.

Rationale: Produce spoils quickly. Singles can't eat large quantities before it spoils.

Major Actions: Consider charging slightly more (not less) for the bulk produce. Singles will pay more knowing they won't have to throw most away.

Tactic Number: 2 **Singled Out**

Tactic: Create a dinner and shopping night. Have a special dinner at your sit-down tables, at a discount when combined with a shopping trip.

Rationale: Singles like to mix meals with other activities especially social occasions.

Major Actions: If you don't have in-store tables, arrange a cooperative promotion with a nearby restaurant.

Tactic Number: 3 **Small, y'all**

Tactic: Keep as many small sizes as possible, with as much variety in flavor as possible. Package or promote multiple flavors together (like Hershey's 4-pack pudding each in a different flavor).

Rationale: Singles can't keep, or don't like to keep, large "family size" containers of product. They do like variety.

Major Actions: Look for higher margins on the small sizes.

Tactic Number: 4 **Gift me more**

Tactic: Have an expanded gift section with upscale chocolates and flower arrangements. Be sure to offer cards, gift wrapping, and even delivery.

Rationale: Singles give more gifts than the average consumer.

Major Actions: Have someone in staff knowledgeable in gifts or consider leasing space to a contractor of higher quality gifts.

☐   Tactic Number: 5 **Rightsized**

Tactic: Have a bulk food section for items like pasta, candies, nuts, coffee, tea, or dried fruit.   Include some upscale products.

Rationale: Rather than taking a low quality/low price position, take a "you are able to buy the right amount for your life style."

Major Actions: Visit some of the bulk food retail stores for merchandising ideas.

☐   Tactic Number: 6 **Broom to grow**

Tactic: Offer housecleaning specials on everything you need to clean your apartment, e.g. for kitchen, bath, living room. Prepackage all items especially for men.

Rationale: Men are less familiar with cleaning (in general), and want a one stop occasion to get what they want.

Major Actions: Ask manufacturers to create pre-wrapped packages targeted to men. Consider merchandising in sections frequently by men.

☐   Tactic Number: 7 **Maid to order**

Tactic: Promote a house cleaning program.   An apartment dweller gets their apartment cleaned by a "cleaning service" one time for free, if the apartment dweller buys an apartment cleaning package.

Rationale: By nature, apartment dwellers feel a bit less "connected" to their residence than those who own a home, and must be encouraged to clean.

Major Actions: Arrange with one of the local cleaning services to do the in-home cleaning. They can use it for leads for future work.

Tactic Number: 8 **Drive sales**

Tactic: Have auto care section specifically for women. Everything they need to keep their cars running and clean. Include in-store information and seminars on how to use your products.

Rationale: Women trust supermarkets and are strangers in the auto parts store. Currently, supermarket auto sections are "masculine".

Major Actions: Create exciting Signage to attract attention, since women will walk by the section without noticing the display.

Tactic Number: 9 **Cookin' with gas!**

Tactic: Have cooking lessons in-store specifically for men. Make it easy to cook, and prepare foods.

Rationale: You can't expect men to buy your products if they don't know what to do with them.

Major Actions: There are numerous cooking schools that would love to "meet" potential new students in a neutral setting where they can show off.

Tactic Number: 10 **Start wining**

Tactic: Merchandise wines in the appropriate food areas. Have white wines in seafood, reds in meats etc.

Rationale: Singles are heavier consumers of alcohol, and use with meals, especially when entertaining.

Major Actions: Look for assistance from the suppliers, in regards to point of sale and informational material.

☐ Tactic Number: 11 **Kits up**

Tactic: Offer "tonight's dinner". Make at least one dinner each night, which is completely available in one place in the store. Microwaveable with entree, vegetables, potato, beverage, dessert. Just let them say "Give me dinner".

Rationale: Singles search for different places to eat and different foods to eat. Everyone tires of pizza and fried chicken.

Major Actions: Reduce as much as possible the number of substitute choices. Don't make a long complicated menu. Simplify it for the single.

☐ Tactic Number: 12 **Nacho night to cook**

Tactic: As it relates to previous tactic, have theme nights for dinner. Every Wednesday is Italian night, every Thursday is "Home Cookin'", every Tuesday is International, etc.

Rationale: Singles will know what to expect for dinner.

Major Actions: Be sure to vary the Italian choice each week. Don't have the same spaghetti and meatballs every Wednesday.

☐ Tactic Number: 13 **Downstream**

Tactic: Offer a dinner and movie promotion, such as "Come in and buy dinner at the supermarket and get your movie free (or reduced price)." Could also offer discounts on streaming services like Netflix and Hulu.

Rationale: Singles love to mix meals with other activities.

Major Actions: Work your promotion with the streaming services. They're not making any money anyway.

Tactic Number: 14 **Not munch going on**

Tactic: Have "After Hours" specials on weekends for meals and snacks, for the singles returning from a night out. Make the promotion begin only after a late hour such as 11:00 PM. Could even operate a food truck outside your store from 11:00PM-3:00AM.

Rationale: Singles often want to eat after a night of clubbing, dancing, or whatever singles do on weekends.

Major Actions: Try a joint promotion at some of the area "hot spots".

Tactic Number: 15 **Picker upper**

Tactic: Offer services such as order online and pickup, package pickup and dry cleaning pickup at reduced rates to those who do their shopping at your store.

Rationale: This service may not be a profit center, but rather will serve singles that use these services more frequently than others. It should draw singles to the store.

Major Actions: Don't just add every possible service, ask single shoppers what services they would value most.

Tactic Number: 16 **Nothin' to lose**

Tactic: Have an expanded weight loss center, and offer an advice telephone # for questions on product use. Include vitamins, exercise products, food supplements, etc. Or, tie in a relationship with a local gym.

Rationale: Singles are frequent users of these products.

Major Actions: Find an area dietitian who will work with you on providing advice. One dietitian can serve a very large region and could work from home.

☐ Tactic Number: 17 **Do you hair me?**

Tactic: Have an expanded personal care section. Tailor it differently for men and women. Include some upscale products.

Rationale: Singles spend more on personal care than their married counterparts.

Major Actions: Try to co-promote with a hair care center or salon, to offer advice and services.

☐ Tactic Number: 18 **You're on my list**

Tactic: Have singles shopping night. Have specials on single-serve products, frozen, and fresh meals.

Rationale: Singles are often looking to meet other singles, why not in a supermarket?

Major Actions: Offer the promotion at times that do not compete with other shoppers. Don't overemphasize the "meeting" aspect. Singles don't want to be forced fed dates, or appear "hungry" (for more than your food).

☐ Tactic Number: 19 **Up the scales**

Tactic: Be sure to include upscale meals and occasionally a little more exotic food in the deli. Don't try to compete on just fast food. Offer something better.

Rationale: Singles can afford to spend a little more on food.

☐ Tactic Number: 20 **Gotta go!**

Tactic: If you're in an urban setting, offer free delivery to apartments and condos. Most have lobbies, so the drop off can be aggregated and quick, and the increased basket size would be worth it.

Rationale: Singles can afford to spend a little more on food, and delivery fits into the single lifestyle.

The Families with Children Target Market

Tactic Number: 21 **We care**

Tactic: Create tie-in programs with local day care programs.

Rationale: Put together a promotion where you support day care programs for parents that support your supermarket. Anything that builds loyalty.

Major Actions: Contact local day care centers. Search for national franchises such as Kinder Care, to reduce number of contacts.

Tactic Number: 22 **Mother of a promotion**

Tactic: Have Mother's Day and Father's Day "I Love You" promotions. The theme would be to have the children write letters as to why they love their mother or why they love their father. These letters could be posted throughout the store with each boy or girl who writes one getting a little gift (e.g. miniature box of candy, etc.) to give to their mother or father.

Rationale: Parents adore these things.

Major Actions: Get with the manufacturers of the products, such as the candies, to have them sponsor these events. They are always looking for opportunities to give away small sample packs of their products.

Tactic Number: 23 **Bumpy ride**

Tactic: Have local police officers give talks on bike safety, and offer free cookies and milk to children who sit through the whole process. Have the children sign bike safety pledge cards and post them around the store.

Rationale: Bike safety is important not only to the children, but especially to the parents, and their being aware of your involvement makes them more comfortable with having your store be their store.

Major Actions: Contact local police chief or community out-reach officer.

Tactic Number: 24 **Put some air in it**

Tactic: Celebrate Bike Safety Week. Have available in the store, a variety of bike riding products such as helmets, water bottles, and reflectors for the bikes

Rationale: Most kids ride bikes, and safety is important to parents. If applicable in your area, ATV safety may also apply.

Major Actions: Contact hard goods buyers to find products.

Tactic Number: 25 **Pennywise now appearing!**

Tactic: Hire local magicians or other entertainers for Saturday afternoon. Put a small stage up in one corner of the parking lot, decorate it, have volunteers to help manage the children and parents can either stay or go in to do their shopping.

Rationale: Anything that can entertain the children while the parents are doing shopping is a contribution to families with children.

Major Actions: Look for entertainers in local apps, or ask at the local high school theater club.

Tactic Number: 26 **Cats up with this one**

Tactic: Have children's pet shows in the parking lot, where the children bring their various pets and display them.

Rationale: Children's pets are important to them, and they love to show them off any place they can. At the same time, pet food is an important part of the total sales of the most supermarkets.

Major Actions: Be sure to make everyone a winner. Arrange with the various pet food manufacturers to sponsor these events and provide you with prizes and discounts, etc. for all the participants.

Tactic Number: 27 **Mack it a sale!**

Tactic: Have truckload sales.

Rationale: Many families with children frequently must buy in larger quantities. Making a fun, exciting process of buying large quantities such as Florida grapefruit sale, Iowa beef sale, or frozen food truckload sale are all ways of creating this kind of fun.

Major Actions: Plan around the first of the month, and try to capture government subsidy (EBT) money at the same time.

Tactic Number: 28 **Not lion about it**

Tactic: Have a parking lot circus.

Rationale: Permit fund raising groups such as the Elks, the Lions, and Kiwanis to set up carnival booths to help raise money for their organizations, and at the same time you can create a good time for the kids.

Major Actions: Since many of the service organizations like the Kiwanis may have booths to raise money, you can also ask them to provide some additional help to supervise and help run the merry-go-round, and things like that so you don't have to use your employees for that part of the business.

Tactic Number: 29 **Infant rice**

Tactic: Newborn promotions

Rationale: Make parents of newborns feel like your supermarket has singled them out as most wanted customers.

Major Actions: Send parents newborn customer packs. Packs would include letters of congratulations, samples of baby-related products and coupons. Work with suppliers for cost-sharing.

Tactic Number: 30 **Home slice**

Tactic: Home Delivery

Rationale: Many split-shift parents, single working mothers, or because of illness, sometimes find it inconvenient to supermarkets. Predictions are 20% of all grocery sales will be online in the next five years.

Major Actions: Subcontract delivery, at least for start-up.

Tactic Number: 31 **Belt it out**

Tactic: Have infant seats and seats belts in shopping carts.

Rationale: Reduce parental stress by allowing parents to make sure their toddlers will not topple out.

Major Actions: Reduce costs by getting suppliers to advertise on seats and straps.

Tactic Number: 32 **No crap**

Tactic: Have conveniently located restrooms (with changing tables).

Rationale: Children always need to go to the bathroom quickly. Extend shopping time and reduce parental stress (and kids too) by having easily accessible, clean restrooms.

Major Actions: Work with suppliers to have samples of bathroom and changing room supplies, e.g., baby wipes, powder and diapers, on hand. Have ample signage, so customers know where the restrooms are located.

Tactic Number: 33 **Ankle breakers**

Tactic: Have kiddie carts (scaled-down versions of the standard shopping carts).

Rationale: Kids can shop with their parents instead of just being passive observers who sooner or later lose patience. This, too, helps reduce injuries because they aren't climbing all over regular-sized carts.

Major Actions: Work with suppliers to help sponsor the carts for on-cart advertising space.

⬜ Tactic Number: 34 **Color me purple**

Tactic: Have coloring boards attached to grocery carts.

Rationale: Provides entertainment while remaining with parents while they shop.

Major Actions: Get suppliers to pay for the boards in return for promotional messages on the coloring boards.

⬜ Tactic Number: 35 **Pizza the pie**

Tactic: Provide samples of items that the kids like, such as pizza, chocolate, flavored milk, and cookies.

Rationale: Help make grocery shopping a festive event for both parents and children. Besides, children are always hungry. This, too, will increase sales of sampled products.

Major Actions: Get suppliers to provide products and personnel.

⬜ Tactic Number: 36 **Seat down!**

Tactic: Install in-store restaurants.

Rationale: Kids (always) and parents (sometimes) are hungry. In-store restaurants can help make shopping a quality time, and will allow parents to complete their shopping.

Major Actions: Table and chairs where families take food purchased from the salad bar and deli. Sub lease space to fast food chain, such as, Taco Bell, Pizza Hut.

Tactic Number: 37 **In play'n sight**

Tactic: Playrooms for kids.

Rationale: Some children are not into shopping. Make sure their parents have ample time to complete their grocery shopping.

Major Actions: Check-out local laws. This one is difficult to implement, as you need people to watch, separate areas for various ages, etc.

Tactic Number: 38 **Not mush time**

Tactic: Permit parents to pre-order regular purchases of infant care products such as disposable diapers, formula, wet wipes, oils, powders and jarred food.

Rationale: These take up so much space in the cart, there is no room for your other products. Additionally, they usually get the same products each week.

Major Actions: Create an order form for the baby supply purchases and distribute them at checkout, or add a spot on your app.

The Health Conscious Target Market

Tactic Number: 39 **Strong sales**

Tactic: Have a complete line of performance-oriented products. These would include high potency vitamins and various protein supplements used by the fitness and athlete types.

Rationale: These are the products that many of the athlete seek to bulk and build up their strength.

Major Actions: Visit the GNC stores, or have an expert in-store, and study the full line of products they carry specifically targeted for the fitness- oriented person.

Tactic Number: 40 **You can weight**

Tactic: Have an expanded section of non-food products for the fitness oriented person. These would include a full line of weights to be carried while walking, fitness devices that you can squeeze to strengthen your wrists and other small, easily stored on the shelf products, which can be used by the fitness fanatic.

Rationale: Fitness people use more than food to obtain their objective.

Major Actions: Look to the manufacturers for help in setting up a section. They would be thrilled to have new channels of distribution.

Tactic Number: 41 **Get the runs**

Tactic: Become a sponsor of the various fitness events which take place in your neighborhood, especially the minor events which are not given the attention of many of the major marathon type races that are held in the area. These could include bicycling clubs, and smaller races that are held.

Major Actions: Find out what all the various groups are in your area and try and join them, get on the email list, have your name listed amongst the membership of the various places so you can be kept abreast of all their events.

☐ Tactic Number: 42 **Hydrate or dydrate**

Tactic: Be sure to have an expanded section of the more obvious fitness related products such as Gatorade in all flavors, 10K drinks, and many of the other products that are available of similar type.

Rationale: Fitness oriented people will let these sections determine where they shop.

Major Actions: Develop signage to get attention.

☐ Tactic Number: 43 **That's a stretch**

Tactic: Offer in-store fitness demos. Get with some of the area fitness programs and ask them to come in and put on special aerobics and fitness demos in the store for the people.

Rationale: It may take more incentive than an expanded health section to get the "hard line" fitness people involved.

Major Actions: Use the parking lot to create more of an event.

☐ Tactic Number: 44 **A great exercise**

Tactic: Offer a complete line of fitness/exercise links on your app or website.

Rationale: Health-oriented shoppers crave information.

Major Actions: Have a special introduction added to your website showing your commitment to the healthy lifestyle.

☐ Tactic Number: 45 **Now weight a minute!**

Tactic: Be sure to offer specials or store coupons or some sort of promotion for products that are frequently bought by fitness fanatics.

Rationale: We tend to overlook these groups when coming up with sales because they are not the main line customer.

Major Actions: Ask manufacturers to contribute to a promotion targeted to the fitness oriented people.

Tactic Number: 46 **You're oh K**

Tactic: Have the 10K jogging events and bicycling events either beginning, or preferably ending, at the supermarket.

Rationale: They are always looking for places to begin and end these races where there are a lot of parking spots and a lot of places to have the participants gather.

Major Actions: Meet with the local bike racing association. They are always looking for new race opportunities.

Tactic Number: 47 **Exercise no caution**

Tactic: Have a page in the weekly circular dedicated to fitness products on sale. This should include both food and non-food items.

Rationale: This will draw attention to your full line of fitness products.

Major Actions: Bring this to the attention of the suppliers, so they will support future sales.

Tactic Number: 48 **Get down to fitness**

Tactic: Advertise in a "special" circular directed to the fitness club members near your store.

Rationale: Fish where the fish are.

Major Actions: Try to arrange a joint event with a fitness club. They are usually looking for an event for their members.

Tactic Number: 49 **In da club**

Tactic: Offer contests for discounts to health and fitness clubs with the purchase of your products.

Rationale: This is a great added value, and the clubs are always looking for new promotions

Major Actions: Contact local health and fitness clubs.

The Health Conscious Target Market

(Health Maintenance)

☐ Tactic Number: 50 **BP me**

Tactic: Have diagnostic devices available at the store free for customer use, including blood pressure machines, scales and cholesterol screening.

Rationale: This group is always looking to monitor their health.

Major Actions: Work with the drug companies to supply both the devices and some training for your staff.

☐ Tactic Number: 51 **Welcome tour store**

Tactic: Offer shopping tours designed for the health maintenance groups.

Rationale: Many of the groups understand the need to monitor their diet to maintain their health condition, however they don't necessarily understand the relationship of all these foods within the stores.

Major Actions: Talk to the local dietitian associations for assistance.

☐ Tactic Number: 52 **Eschew the fat**

Tactic: Get with many of the manufacturers that have low sodium, low fat or other health products available to sponsor a "healthy eating" page of your weekly circular, or on your website.

Rationale: Targeted themes in the circular have far more impact on a targeted consumer than having the items spread throughout the circular.

☐ Tactic Number: 53 **I'm lipid!**

Tactic: Have regular cholesterol testing done within the supermarket.

Rationale: Cholesterol is a major concern in America today and of many consumers WITHOUT a cholesterol problem. Many of the people in your supermarket are not spending money on meat and other products because they fear that they may have high fat and cholesterol intakes.

Major Actions: Contact your public health department.

Tactic Number: 54 **On one condition**

Tactic: Maintain a full set of pamphlets, brochures and other reputable materials that discuss health conditions in the book and magazine section of your store.

Rationale: People in this group are knowledge seekers.

Major Actions: Show you are a partner in a "whole health" solution for any health maintenance customers.

Tactic Number: 55 **Counter argument**

Tactic: Maintain a complete and full line of over the counter (OTC) vitamins, mineral supplements, nutritional supplements, homeopathic solutions, and other food related health foods.

Rationale: This group uses more supplements than the average consumer.

Major Actions: Contact vitamin manufacturers for special displays.

Tactic Number: 56 **Healthy profits**

Tactic: Have health promotion days. These would be certain events where you bring in the Dairy Council or the American Heart Association to host "good eating day".

Rationale: This makes an event out of your commitment to health maintenance.

Major Actions: All the groups that sponsor good health and healthy eating usually have outreach programs that are free, or virtually free.

Tactic Number: 57 **Tour of duty**

Tactic: Offer store tours to eat healthy. Local dietitians would be happy to run these types of tours for free, or a very small fee.

Rationale: People in this group want to do as many things as they can to stay healthy.

Major Actions: Contact your local Dietetic Association or Dairy Council.

Tactic Number: 58 **Healthy idea**

Tactic: Have the name of a consulting dietitian available for contact from your customers to answer questions with respect to their good eating.

Rationale: So many customer questions will be complex and you won't have qualified personnel available to answer them.

Major Actions: Either have a "go to" dietitian, or some reliable and verifiably factual websites to consult.

Tactic Number: 59 **Can't be beat**

Tactic: Have a Healthy Heart Day, or similar events, sponsored by the local chapter of the American Heart Association, the American Diabetes Association, etc. Donate some percent of your proceeds for that day's sales.

Rationale: Usually people with these conditions are quite involved with these organizations and your demonstration of support of them is very important.

Major Actions: Contact the local chapters of these organizations and plan event days. These organizations are always looking for ways to not only raise money but create awareness for the problem.

Tactic Number: 60 **Oily in the day**

Tactic: Offer cooking classes specifically targeted for certain conditions, for example cooking for a healthy heart, or cooking with low salt and making great meals.

Rationale: In many cases, much of the prepared food which you sell will not be acceptable to these customers. And, these customers are going to be required to prepare most of their own food.

Major Actions: Almost all the major associations affiliated with these diseases and conditions have cookbooks and things available for you.

Tactic Number: 61 **Book it**

Tactic: Have an expanded "cooking healthy" section on your website or app. Sell cookbooks, or have a vibrant YouTube channel for eating healthier.

Rationale: Where else to find a cookbook but in a food store?

Tactic Number: 62 **Heart evidence**

Tactic: Advertise in many of the local brochures of the health organizations that are available to the consumer. For example, most of the major associations such as the American Heart Association and fitness groups have newsletters, etc.

Rationale: If you have a close relationship with those local organizations, they will permit you to advertise and contribute to their newsletter.

Tactic Number: 63 **Lettuce dine**

Tactic: Have a produce sale tied in with the "5 a Day" for healthy eating theme.

Rationale: You can take advantage of significant advertising of this program by the produce growers.

The Health Conscious Target Market

(Health Condition)

Tactic Number: 64 **No, sugar**

Tactic: Offer shopping tours designed for specific health conditions such as diabetes, high blood pressure, etc.

Rationale: Many of the people in these groups understand the need to monitor their diet to maintain their health condition, however they don't necessarily understand the relationship of all these foods within the stores.

Major Actions: Talk to the local dietitian associations for assistance.

Tactic Number: 65 **Are you sure, bro?**

Tactic: Distribute pamphlets and brochures available from pharmaceutical companies that discuss the various health conditions.

Rationale: People with these conditions are avid readers of this type of material.

Major Actions: Approach your suppliers of pharmaceuticals and ask them for consumer oriented materials. All the pharmaceutical manufacturers will have these materials available for you to put out.

Tactic Number: 66 **No pressure**

Tactic: Offer drug monitoring programs for people who take chronic disease pharmaceuticals, such as those with hypertension, etc. Since you will be filling most of the prescriptions, you will know whether the time has come for them to be refilled and if the customer has come back.

Rationale: These people may forget and are very good customers.

Major Actions: Consider a computerized calling system, or auto-refill.

☐ Tactic Number: 67 **All night with me**

Tactic: If your supermarket pharmacy is not open 24 hours, be sure to give those customers who buy the prescription pharmaceuticals from your pharmacy an emergency number where they can call any time for their prescriptions.

Rationale: Emergencies happen.

Major Actions: While many people think that it's going to be a bit of an inconvenience to have customers calling at all hours for a prescription, keep in mind that your customers also do not like to go to the pharmacy at 4:00 am on Sunday.

☐ Tactic Number: 68 **Well conditioned**

Tactic: Be sure to offer specials or store coupons, or some sort of promotion, for products that are frequently bought by people with chronic diseases (conditions).

Rationale: These people are in your store all the time, and these are the products that are important to them. Whereas it wouldn't make sense to target such products in general supermarkets because of their low frequency of purchase, in supermarkets targeted to the disease prevention people, it makes very good sense.

Major Actions: Be sure to contact the manufacturers of these products and ask them to participate in an exciting promotion for people that have these kinds of conditions.

☐ Tactic Number: 69 **Salt of the earth**

Tactic: Group together all dietetic products, such as low salt or low sugar products, etc. for people with specific conditions. Even consider a section for hypertensives or diabetics.

Rationale: Don't make people search the entire store for products they need for their condition.

Tactic Number: 70 **Doctor in the house**

Tactic: Develop a special brochure that can be placed in physicians' offices explaining that your store is there to serve their dietary needs.

Rationale: Physicians hate to discuss this with patients anyway.

Major Actions: Work with your pharmaceutical detail rep to assist in distributing the brochures.

Tactic Number: 71 **I carry about you**

Tactic: Offer a bagging service, a "carry to your car" service or a specialized home delivery service to those people that are in a condition that carrying heavy bags or pushing heavy carts may impact their health.

Rationale: Sick people, or people with certain conditions, may need more help; but CAUTION: if you offer persons a special card to allow them access to the service, it shouldn't have any negative indication on it such as "Sick Person", simply our "Special Customer" card would be appropriate.

Tactic Number: 72 **Back to the pharm**

Tactic: Have a complete and expanded pharmacy within the store.

Rationale: Many people are required to take an assortment of prescription drugs for these and chronic conditions and diseases.

Tactic Number: 73 **It's only natural**

Tactic: Have a complete line of organic food, and other health foods.

Rationale: This group sees organic as pure. These products also have a much higher margin.

☐ Tactic Number: 74 **I herb you!**

Tactic: Have part of the pharmacy related to homeopathic type products such as medicinal herbs, and other similar products.

Rationale: People involved in natural foods are often more likely to be involved with non-traditional medicine.

☐ Tactic Number: 75 **How it pans out**

Tactic: Have a complete line of cookbooks oriented to this group, including eating healthy, low fat cooking, and the joys of vegetarianism, or macrobiotic cooking.

Rationale: Many people are just beginning this phase of their eating, and are looking for ways to prepare food differently.

The
Health
Conscious
Target Market

(Natural Food Advocates)

☐ Tactic Number: **76 Not mush room in here**

Tactic: Offer classes for cooking with fresh vegetables, and macrobiotic cooking.

Rationale: This group enjoys having control over the foods they eat, and much of the prepared foods you sell may not be acceptable to them.

Major Actions: Look for authors of cookbooks for help.

☐ Tactic Number: **77 The author ones**

Tactic: Have book signings and cooking classes by the authors of the natural cookbooks.

Rationale: Authors (other than top 10 leading authors) are always looking for a chance to merchandise their books.

Major Actions: Contact publishing houses for authors of natural food cook books.

☐ Tactic Number: **78 Simple truths**

Tactic: Include in your snack food sections, assortments of products that would meet this group's needs, such as fresh produce, granola bars, simple ingredient foods, and fresh trail mix in the snack section.

Rationale: Demonstrate to this group that you understand that these are snacks that are part of their everyday eating habits.

☐ Tactic Number: **79 New deli**

Tactic: Offer in your deli section fresh prepared foods which meet this groups requirements, such as vegetable dishes, etc.

Rationale: In many cases, the prepared foods in the deli case are targeted to the typical customer, and not the natural food buff.

Tactic Number: 80 **You look radishing!**

Tactic: Be sure to have an assortment of products in your salad bar such as low fat salad dressings and organic produce in the salad bar. Consider an organic salad bar.

Rationale: Natural food consumer are under time pressures, too.

Tactic Number: 81 **Let's vegan again**

Tactic: Offer promotions and sales on products targeted to this group. Have a vegetarian sale.

Rationale: Sales are almost always on traditional products.

Major Actions: Get with the local suppliers to put on such an event.

Tactic Number: 82 **A farmer employee**

Tactic: In good weather conditions, set up your produce stand outside, make it look like a farm stand.

Rationale: In many cases, the shopper tends to feel that this kind of outdoor farmer's market is fresher or is better.

Tactic Number: 83 **Romaine the leader**

Tactic: Have a wide range of produce available.

Rationale: People choose stores to buy all their foods where they believe they have products that meet their needs. Even though those products are not purchased with great frequency, it is the drawing card that gets them into the store.

Tactic Number: 84 **Zucchini do anything**

Tactic: Do not have a separate section called "Health Foods", because those products indicate that somehow this is a small section for just a few people. Integrate your foods throughout the whole store so that the shopper feels as if they are part of the whole shopping experience.

Rationale: Natural food consumers don't like to see their eating habits labels "special" or "unusual."

☐ Tactic Number: 85 **Well, well, well**

Tactic: Offer healthy recipes. These can be distributed throughout the store in the various sections of the store. Included with this would be free literature from places like the American Heart Association.

Rationale: Although these consumers are not health "freaks", they have a higher interest in the relationship of food and health.

☐ Tactic Number: 86 **De tour starts here**

Tactic: Offer health tours of the supermarket which can be conducted by dietitians or home economists who will talk about the various products in the store and the advantages and disadvantages of all of them.

Rationale: These consumers are always looking for new information.

The
Ethnic Group
Target Market

(African Americans)

☐ Tactic Number: 87 **Get fishy with it**

Tactic: Have an expanded seafood section including products such as Catfish, Bluefish, Spot, and Ocean Perch.

Rationale: These items are popular among African Americans.

Major Actions: Consider selling these products in your canned food and frozen food sections, as well as in the fresh seafood section.

☐ Tactic Number: 88 **R-e-s-p-e-c-t**

Tactic: Train your employees to respect all customers.

Rationale: Studies indicate that African Americans place a greater value on the friendliness of employees than Caucasian shoppers do.

Major Actions: Contact your local NAACP or other similar organization to provide guidance.

☐ Tactic Number: 89 **Kale yeah!**

Tactic: Expand the assortment in your produce section to include products such as collard greens, kale, okra, and mustard greens.

Rationale: These products are popular among African Americans.

☐ Tactic Number: 90 **Game theory**

Tactic: Sponsor local youth sporting event/cultural activities with groups such as the Police Athletic League.

Rationale: PAL and other organizations are always looking for sponsors. All teens need programs of this type to keep them occupied. Many African-American youths don't have the same opportunity as other groups.

◻ Tactic Number: 91 **Let's meat in the back aisle**

Tactic: Expand your meat department to include ham hocks, pig's feet, chitterlings, turkey and chicken parts and other non-traditional meats which are popular among African Americans.

Rationale: These products are popular among African Americans.

◻ Tactic Number: 92 **Group on!**

Tactic: Offer travel service discounts.

Rationale: Studies indicate that African Americans like to travel in groups or with the entire family. Travel is an important social/family function.

Major Actions: You could organize group rate travel destinations.

◻ Tactic Number: 93 **Cue it up**

Tactic: Have an expanded cuts and types of meats that are best barbecued.

Rationale: BBQ is a popular method of cooking among African Americans. This type of cross merchandising can increase sales of BBQ items and meat products.

Major Actions: Look to have parking lot sales with a working "pit" on the site.

◻ Tactic Number: 94 **A lot of meat!**

Tactic: Sponsor a BBQ in your parking lot during the summer months.

Rationale: Special events like these are an excellent way not only to give something back to your customers, but you can benefit by sampling new products.

☐ Tactic Number: 95 **Book it!**

Tactic: During Black History Month, sell books about Black history along with a food purchase.

Rationale: African Americans want to see that you are committed to their interests as well as their money.

☐ Tactic Number: 96 **Go traditional**

Tactic: Celebrate important African American holidays, such as Kwanzaa.

Rationale: These traditional holidays are becoming more important to the African American culture.

Major Actions: Contact the local organizations to find out how you can help celebrate the holidays in store.

☐ Tactic Number: 97 **Shopping music**

Tactic: Play music on in-store radio popular with all ethnicities, paying attention to preferences that can go across all shoppers.

Rationale: Like any subculture, people feel more at home when the music they like is playing.

Major Actions: Create a consumer committee to select the music.

☐ Tactic Number: 98 **Safety counts!**

Tactic: Sponsor anti-violence programs, to be viewed as part of the solution for issues in society.

Rationale: Help to make your neighborhood a safer place, you may even be saving lives.

Major Actions: Contact your local police or government agency.

☐ Tactic Number: 99 **Queue the cue**

Tactic: During the summer months, have one single section where your customers can buy all their BBQ needs.

Rationale: Barbecuing is a popular form of cooking among African Americans. In addition to placing charcoal, lighter fluid (etc.) in this section. Consider cross merchandising sauces, soda, chips, etc. there.

Major Actions: Have contests between stores to see who can create the best section.

☐ Tactic Number: 100 **Hair me now**

Tactic: Have a complete section of beauty care targeted to African Americans. In larger retailers, the majority of the sets will not cover the needs of the African American.

The Ethnic Group Target Market

(Italians)

Tactic Number: 101 **Ice to have**

Tactic: During the warmer months consider selling traditional, gourmet Italian water ice, rather than the variety sold in the frozen food sections.

Rationale: This is popular with a wider group of consumers than just Italians.

Major Actions: There are numerous water ice suppliers.

Tactic Number: 102 **Oh, prosciutto**

Tactic: Carry a wide variety of Italian meats and cheeses in the deli section.

Rationale: Traditional meats and cheeses are important aspects of Italian cuisine, and will entice your target market to shop at your store.

Tactic Number: 103 **Pastabilities**

Tactic: Hire an authentic Italian chef to prepare quality dishes and sauces, which could be taken home.

Rationale: This has been very successful for restaurants.

Major Actions: Make sure the sauces and dishes are both tasty and genuinely Italian dishes. Your target market may not be willing to buy them otherwise.

Tactic Number: 104 **Oily in the day**

Tactic: Carry a wide variety of high quality Italian olive oil in your store.

Rationale: Olive oil plays a large role in authentic Italian cuisine. Offering high quality, authentic Italian olive oil will appeal to your target market.

Major Actions: Be sure you understand these are on the shelf to communicate commitment to the target market and not just sales. Don't evaluate program's success on sales of less popular olive oils.

☐   Tactic Number: 105 **Getting' saucy**

Tactic: Offer the highest quality and widest variety of tomatoes in your produce department.

Rationale: The tomato is an essential part of the Italian diet.

Major Actions: Contact specialty suppliers. Many Italians prefer to make sauces and other dishes from scratch. Offering high quality tomatoes will attract your target customers.

☐   Tactic Number: 106 **La festa**

Tactic: Sponsor community festivals, such as the annual St. Anthony's Festival in Wilmington, Delaware, or "Night in Venice" Festival in Ocean City, New Jersey or other regional events.

Rationale: This is an excellent way to have your store's name associated with traditional Italian events.

Major Actions: Contact the local city halls to see what ethnic events are coming up. Since many of the Italian events are associated with the church, look at the church calendar.

☐   Tactic Number: 107 **Mangiamo**

Tactic: Announce in-store advertisement in both English and Italian. In-store fliers, and window signage should also be bilingual.

Rationale: Even though most Italians speak perfect English, the Italian signage makes your target customers feel welcomed.

Major Actions: Hire local customers to translate your advertisements into Italian.

Tactic Number: 108 **Picture this**

Tactic: Use the design of your store (i.e. flags, pictures, etc.) to remind your customers of their homeland.

Rationale: By reminding your customers about "home", and by making it clear you recognize their Italian heritage, you can make them feel comfortable about shopping in your store.

Tactic Number: 109 **Adagio**

Tactic: Play traditional Italian music in your store.

Rationale: This will make your Italian customers feel at home. Everyone loves familiar music!

Major Actions: Contact your in-store music supplier or create your own tracks.

Tactic Number: 110 **Cibo**

Tactic: Have a wide variety of cookbooks with traditional Italian recipes available in your store.

Rationale: Cookbooks are popular with this subgroup.

Tactic Number: 111 **Grazie. Prego.**

Tactic: Advertise on Italian radio stations in the area.

Rationale: If your target market is Italian speaking, it is a safe bet that many listen to such a station.

Major Actions: This is an excellent way to reach your target market, and get your message across. You may consider a mix between an Italian and English advertisement.

☐ Tactic Number: 112 **It's on aisle 8, capisci?**

Tactic: Hire employees who speak both English and Italian.

Rationale: This will allow your employees to communicate better with your customer, and vice versa.

Major Actions: Contact local Italian American Clubs for potential employees and post signs for employment at their meeting halls.

☐ Tactic Number: 113 **Don't tell mamma**

Tactic: Prepare your own tomato sauce/gravy, which your customers can purchase. Offer free samples, so your customers can know that it is a quality sauce using only the finest ingredients.

Rationale: This should be popular with all customers in your store.

Major Actions: Consult with authentic Italian chef for a recipe that can be produced in bulk.

☐ Tactic Number: 114 **Sleeping with the fishes**

Tactic: Be sure to carry all the fish products for the traditional Italian Christmas Eve dinner, including antipasto and Italian cookies.

Rationale: You want your Italian customers to believe that your store is for all their needs, not just the ones that are convenient for you to carry.

☐ Tactic Number: 115 **Start wining!**

Tactic: Stock a wide variety of hard to find wines imported from Italy.

Rationale: Most stores don't have a wide assortment of Italian wines, because they are less popular with the American consumer than California or French wines.

Tactic Number: 116 **Fish Fryday!**

Tactic: Offer seafood specials on Fridays, especially during Lent.

Rationale: Many Italians are also Catholic, and are accustomed to eating fish instead of meat on Fridays, especially during Lent.

Tactic Number: 117 **Itsa sagra!**

Tactic: Sponsor an Italian cooking contest.

Rationale: Most Italians are proud of their cuisine and their personal cooking ability. A contest such as this will allow your customers to have some fun, and it shows them that you appreciate their talent and want others to recognize them.

Major Actions: You could make this contest a regular event. Post the winner's picture and recipe in the front of the store. Reward the winner with cash prizes.

Tactic Number: 118 **A good habit**

Tactic: Advertise in the local Catholic church bulletin.

Rationale: Although all Italians are not Catholic, most are.

Major Actions: Contact the local church, to place advertisements.

Tactic Number: 119 **Time to Rome**

Tactic: Sponsor a contest (of some kind), where the grand prize is a trip to Italy.

Rationale: This shows your customers that you are aware of their heritage, and want the winner of your contest to be able to visit the "old country."

Major Actions: Contact a local travel agent or get help for your advertising. Co-promote with a manufacturer of an Italian food supplier.

☐ Tactic Number: 120 **The yeast you can do**

Tactic: Offer Italian bread every day in your bakery.
Rationale: Bread plays a very important part in the Italian diet. Fresh bread, of good quality, will attract your target market.
`
Major Actions: If you don't bake in-store, have a local bakery supplier.

☐ Tactic Number: 121 **Altar the calendar**

Tactic: Sponsor local Catholic church events, such as the Carnivals.

Rationale: This will show commitment to organizations important to the target audience.

☐ Tactic Number: 122 **That's radicchious**

Tactic: Carry traditional Italian produce, such as radicchio and Italian parsley, and broccoli rabe.

Rationale: Produce section often influences whether customers will shop in a store. Having produce specifically targeted to Italians will increase their chance of shopping in your store.

The Ethnic Group Target Market

(Jewish)

☐ Tactic Number: 123 **Parve for the course**

Tactic: Develop and implement an in-store shelf label system that easily identifies the kosher or parve products at their shelf location, as a part of the regular label information.

Rationale: Customers of the Jewish descent, especially orthodox and conservative sects, tend to buy based upon their strict dietary laws; which prohibit certain ingredients, fats and packaging techniques. This shelf label system would also help Muslims, vegetarians and Seventh Day Adventists, and other non-Jewish store customers, that seek the kosher label for its mark of quality, parity and wholesomeness.

Major Actions: This may be done by means of a symbol or a color, or some other distinguishing means

☐ Tactic Number: 124 **Ko sher we carry that**

Tactic: Develop a separate circular, or a section within the current circular, devoted to products targeted to and consumed by Jewish customers. This can be done via the loyalty data of the store, to allow precision targeting at the store or market area level.

Rationale: Most circulars are mass market oriented, and often developed based upon manufacturer trade promotion dollars. They tend to be more generalized in nature, than specifically targeted.

Major Actions: Contact suppliers of kosher products to participate in circular.

☐ Tactic Number: 125 **Do you mine?**

Tactic: Using loyalty card data, or by simply asking the customer if they follow kosher guidelines, implement separating and bagging kosher foods in separate carry out bags from non-kosher foods. Kosher food can go into a specially designed and printed bag, especially at the holidays.

Rationale: This acknowledgment of the Jewish customer's requirements, and the education of cashiers and baggers, validates the importance and uniqueness of the customer.

Major Actions: Contact the synagogue to determine the guidelines. Also, note that contacting the Rabbi will provide some public relations value.

☐ Tactic Number: 126 **Consumer packaged good**

Tactic: Replace current packaging materials, which are not kosher, with kosher packaging materials for all in-store packaged foods from the deli, food court for takeout and refrigerated case for foodservice/deli microwavable takeout items.

Rationale: Allows kosher items to remain kosher, even when heated in a non-kosher oven.

Major Actions: Contact your packaging suppliers.

☐ Tactic Number: 127 **I gefilte left out**

Tactic: Install as a new offering, or replace your current non-kosher in-store rotisserie chicken program, with a kosher certified rotisserie chicken program.

Rationale: Chicken and rotisserie chicken are a strong category and foodservice concept, respectively in supermarkets. Consumers, both Jewish and non-Jewish, have more confidence in the kosher seal of approval. It is viewed as having integrity and assures purity, quality and wholesomeness. Kosher is meaningful to non-Jewish customers, thereby enhancing the in-store chicken program, while allowing Jewish consumers and consumers looking for the kosher seal and the opportunity to purchase in-store chicken.

Major Actions: Contact your poultry supplier and Rabbi to verify the cooking process follows kosher rules.

☐ Tactic Number: 128 **Brisket business today**

Tactic: Create a Kosher deli, to replace the current in-store deli, in those stores with above average Jewish customer indexes in the market trade area.

Rationale: Kosher means cleanliness and high or higher standard of quality and manufacturing control than non-Kosher, even among non-Jewish consumers. The store can leverage this and use it to position the store for both the target market consumer, Jewish, as well as customers wishing the higher level of quality and ethnic variety that can be merchandised through real Jewish deli.

☐ Tactic Number: 129 **Challah at me**

Tactic: Certify the in-store bakery as Kosher, and undertake promotions and merchandising efforts to inform and educate both non-Jewish and Jewish customers about the quality and cleanliness implications.

Rationale: Allows the store to capture Jewish customers' purchases while positioning the Kosher program as a quality advantage for the benefit of all customers of the store. The promotion will demystify the Kosher label, and move it from a religious and cultural word not usually understood by Christians, to more of a food preparation, quality and cleanliness issue linked to the store for all customers.

☐ Tactic Number: 130 **Lox to think about**

Tactic: Provide takeout Kosher prepared holiday meals for the Jewish religious holy days such as Passover, Rosh Hashanah, Yom Kippur, and Hanukkah that meet all the religious Kosher standards, while still being high in quality, tasty, and traditional recipes offering convenience.

Rationale: Like other customers, time saving and convenient high quality holiday meals and foods are desirable, especially at holidays. Food is so much a part of the religious, cultural, and family experience of the moment. This type of product and services offering will broaden the customer perception of the store as valuing their business and being able to be of help at a time may be critical.

☐ Tactic Number: 131 **Latke customers in here**

Tactic: Develop a database within your current frequent shopper program or, if you do not have one of those, start a database of your Jewish customers that will allow you to communicate and track purchase behavior and patterns.

Rationale: Most efforts to date have been very one-way in orientation and direction of benefits - to the store! This would allow stores with higher indexes of Jewish in the market area to develop precision target marketing efforts based upon actual purchase and customer behavior.

☐ Tactic Number: 132 **Can't Passover this offer**

Tactic: Stimulate Jewish customer awareness of your store as their store by use of your database or by the store circular (preferably a precision target marketing database technique) to build store traffic ad sales. Come to your store for your Jewish holiday shopping needs, and bring this notice with you for a free gift, i.e. a bottle of Passover wine.

Rationale: Reward loyalty of those Jewish customers who have shopped regularly at your store, and show your appreciation in a precision target marketing way.

☐ Tactic Number: 133 **Babka for apples**

Tactic: Stores can purchase and merchandise more Israeli-sourced products. Stores can also tailor the traditional "register tapes for charity or schools" or "labels for equipment" programs to target the Jewish consumers' loyalties, by customizing such programs.

Rationale: Store loyalty and manufacturer brand loyalty programs have already been shown to work. Affinity programs for loyalty to both Israel and their temple of worship, or other Jewish charities, could be very effective as an ongoing program for a store.

The
Ethnic Group
Target Market

(Muslim)

Tactic Number: 134 **Permit me to show you**

Tactic: Develop and implement an in-store shelf label system that easily identifies the halal products at their shelf location, as a part of the regular label information.

Rationale: Customers of the Muslim religion, tend to buy based upon their strict dietary laws; which prohibit certain ingredients, fats and packaging techniques. Halal translates into "permissible", and is strictly followed by many Muslims

Major Actions: This may be done by means of a symbol or a color, or some other distinguishing means

Tactic Number: 135 **Oh, of couscous we have that**

Tactic: Develop a separate circular, or a section within the current circular, devoted to products targeted to and consumed by Muslim customers. This can be done via the loyalty data of the store, to allow precision targeting at the store or market area level.

Rationale: Most circulars are mass market oriented, and often developed based upon manufacturer trade promotion dollars. They tend to be more generalized in nature, than specifically targeted.

Major Actions: Contact suppliers of halal products to participate in circular.

Tactic Number: 136 **Time to goat**

Tactic: Use loyalty card data, or by simply asking the customer if they follow Muslim guidelines and lifestyle, and bag their products separately from non-compliant products. Muslims are not allowed to consume alcohol, pig meat, meat of an animal that has died of natural causes (or, as a result of strangling or beating), or blood in liquid form.

Rationale: This acknowledgment of the Muslim customer's requirements, and the education of cashiers and baggers, validates the importance and uniqueness of the customer.

Major Actions: Contact the mosques to determine the guidelines. Also, note that contacting the Imam will provide some public relations value.

☐ Tactic Number: 137 **What's saffr on the menu?**

Tactic: Replace current packaging materials, which are not halal, with clearly marked packaging materials for all in-store packaged foods from the deli, food court for takeout and refrigerated case for foodservice/deli microwavable takeout items.

Rationale: Allows halal items to remain halal even when heated in a non-halal oven.

Major Actions: Contact your packaging suppliers.

☐ Tactic Number: 138 **Cumin on in**

Tactic: Install as a new offering, or replace your current non-halal in-store rotisserie chicken program, with a halal certified rotisserie chicken program.

Rationale: Chicken and rotisserie chicken are a strong category and foodservice concept, respectively in supermarkets. Consumers, both Muslim and non-Muslim, have more confidence in the halal seal of approval. It is viewed as having integrity and assures purity, quality and wholesomeness.

Major Actions: Contact your poultry supplier and Imam to verify the cooking process follows halal rules.

☐ Tactic Number: 139 **No porkin' good**

Tactic: Understand the other items avoided by Muslim customers, and respect their faith in store set-up, as much as you can while not isolating other non-Muslim customers.

Rationale: Some Muslims also avoid cakes, biscuits or ice-cream containing animal-based products such as lard, gelatin or enzymes, and packaged foods that contain animal fat- in case it comes from pigs.

Tactic Number: 140 **Wheat better do this**

Tactic: Certify the in-store bakery as halal, and undertake promotions and merchandising efforts to inform and educate both non-Muslim and Muslim customers about the implications.

Rationale: Allows the store to capture Muslim customers' purchases while positioning the halal program as a quality advantage for the benefit of all customers of the store. The promotion will demystify the halal label, and move it from a religious and cultural word not usually understood by Christians, to more of a food preparation, quality and cleanliness issue linked to the store for all customers.

Tactic Number: 141 **Recipe for success**

Tactic: Provide takeout halal prepared holiday meals for the Muslim religious holy days such as Eid Al-Fitr and Eid Al-Adha that meet all the religious halal standards, while still being high in quality, tasty, and traditional recipes offering convenience.

Rationale: Food is so much a part of the religious, cultural, and family experience of the moment. Eid Al-Fitr is celebrated at the end Ramadan (a month of fasting during daylight hours). The Eid Al-Fitr celebration begins with prayers the morning of Shawal, and is followed by breakfast, and often celebratory meals throughout the day. Eid Al-Adha is celebrated on the tenth day of Dhu Al-Hijah, when pilgrimage takes place, and lasts for four days.

Tactic Number: 142 **That's a mezze data**

Tactic: Develop a database within your current frequent shopper program or, if you do not have one of those, start a database of your Muslim customers that will allow you to communicate and track purchase behavior and patterns.

Rationale: Most efforts to date have been very one-way in orientation and direction of benefits - to the store! This would allow stores with higher indexes of Muslims in the market area to develop precision target marketing efforts based upon actual purchase and customer behavior.

☐   Tactic Number: 143 **On the lamb**

Tactic: Stimulate Muslim customer awareness of your store as their store by use of your database or by the store circular (preferably a precision target marketing database technique) to build store traffic ad sales. Come to your store for your Muslim holiday shopping needs, and bring this notice with you for a free gift, i.e. a halal chicken or cut of lamb.

Rationale: Reward loyalty of those Muslim customers who have shopped regularly at your store, and show your appreciation in a precision target marketing way.

☐   Tactic Number: 144 **Produce results**

Tactic: As with all customers, ensure your produce department is supremely fresh, and has the assortment needed by Muslim customers.

Rationale: Vegetables, fruits and grains are halal in themselves, and are a large portion of the Muslim diet. As for animal-derived foods, eggs and milk are halal. This means most vegetarian dishes are halal.

The
Ethnic Group
Target Market

(Germans)

☐ Tactic Number: 145 **Not mis-construdeled**

Tactic: Have your bakery specialize in uniquely German breads and pastries, such as strudels.

Rationale: Baked products are an important part of the German diet.

☐ Tactic Number: 146 **It's the wurst**

Tactic: Have a German sausage master make sausage in your store. Do this at least on special occasions, if not more regularly, like every Wednesday.

Rationale: This is typical in Germany, and you can offer your customers something they can't get at another store.

Major Actions: Contact the local German-American society.

☐ Tactic Number: 147 **You have to give a schnitzel**

Tactic: Offer an extended variety of traditional bratwursts and schnitzels in your meat department.

Rationale: This is commonplace in every German food store.

☐ Tactic Number: 148 **Currywurst is best**

Tactic: Import hard to find German products.

Rationale: These products will add to your store, and be an excellent way to attract your German customers.

Major Actions: Contact specialty suppliers, such as UNFI.

☐ Tactic Number: 149 **In the Bach aisle**

Tactic: Play traditional German music in your store.

Rationale: This will appeal to your customers, and make his or her shopping experience more enjoyable.

Major Actions: Create your own mix, or buy traditional music.

☐ Tactic Number: 150 **Don't be a sauerbraten**

Tactic: Have a storyteller come in and tell traditional German folk stories to children of traditional German customers.

Rationale: This will appeal to the children of your target market. It will encourage the parents to patronize your store, as the children will have something to do while they shop in your store.

Major Actions: Contact the local German-American Society for assistance.

☐ Tactic Number: 151 **Munchen on this!**

Tactic: Decorate your store with German flags, pictures of Germany, and so forth.

Rationale: This shows your commitment to your German customers.

Major Actions: Ask local travel agencies or airlines for posters of Germany. Also, check with suppliers of imported products for posters.

☐ Tactic Number: 152 **Not too krauted**

Tactic: Have a weekly seminar in your store, which demonstrates how to prepare traditional German dishes.

Rationale: Many of your customers may be interested in cooking traditional German dishes, but they may not know how.

Major Actions: Find a couple Germans who shop in your store, and ask them to plan the seminars. You most likely won't have to pay them, just let them keep the products.

☐   Tactic Number: 153 **Let's brotchen this topic**

Tactic: Distribute pamphlets with recipes for traditional German dishes.

Rationale: These can be in concert with the in-store recipes.

☐   Tactic Number: 154 **Sprechen sie groceries?**

Tactic: Hire employees who speak both German and English.

Rationale: This will make it easier for those customers who are not comfortable conversing and asking questions in English.

☐   Tactic Number: 155 **I love your Cologne**

Tactic: Sell wine and schnapps imported from Germany in your beer and wine departments.   Carry actual authentic kolsch from Cologne.

Rationale: Most wine and beer sections are stocked with California and French wines, and American beers.   Germans love German wines. Schnapps is very common on food market shelves.

Major Actions: Contact   your   alcohol   distributors   for selections.

☐   Tactic Number: 156 **A Bavaria good time**

Tactic: Sponsor a contest where the grand prize is a trip to Germany.

Rationale: This is one way to attract customers, and show them that you are keenly aware of their German heritage.

Major Actions: Contact local travel agency or airline for assistance.

☐ Tactic Number: 157 **Polka fun at me**

Tactic: Have a German day in your store. Consider hiring a musician or a band to play traditional music and to sing songs. Rationale: This is a good way to get your target market to come to your store and enjoy themselves.

Major Actions: While they are there, give away samples of traditional German foods and distribute coupons for products which are on special.

☐ Tactic Number: 158 **You look Fasching today**

Tactic: Sponsor food festivals along with German - American groups.

Rationale: The sponsorship of food festivals, which are specifically geared towards German – Americans, is an excellent way to reach your target market.

The Ethnic Group Target Market

(Hispanic)

☐ Tactic Number: 159 **Si the sign**

Tactic: Have all signage in the store in both English and Spanish.

Rationale: Many Hispanics have Spanish as their only language, and those who speak English find it respectful that signs are also in Spanish.

Major Actions: Meet with manufacturers to assist in creating Spanish signs. Don't just use magic marker on cardboard. Do it right.

☐ Tactic Number: 160 **Peppered with variety**

Tactic: Include in the produce section those kinds of products that are attractive to the Hispanic consumer. These may vary by the type of Hispanic shopping at your store, e.g. Mexican, Cuban, etc.

Rationale: Although these products may not be high volume purchases, they are the things which the Hispanic community uses to choose the store they will shop in.

Major Actions: Go to Hispanic bodegas to see the selections of produce.

☐ Tactic Number: 161 **Make a special Ariel for them**

Tactic: Be sure to offer brands that are commonplace in their home countries.

Rationale: Many stores carry the available American brands for Hispanics, but only a few will have the national brands. Their brands from home.

Major Actions: Call specialty distributors for available brands, and ask your shoppers what brands they would like, or the brands they miss the most.

☐   Tactic Number: 162 **Te amo, customers**

Tactic: Offer services in the same fashion that Hispanics are offered in their home country. For example, if some products are sold via the service counter rather than self-service, you should sell it over the service counter.

Rationale: It makes your customers feel at home.

Major Actions: Have focus groups with your Hispanic shoppers and ask them about the supermarkets at home. How is your store different?

☐   Tactic Number: 163 **Comestibles especiales aqui**

Tactic: Have all website material and circulars available in English and Spanish.

Rationale: Many Hispanics have Spanish as their only language, and those who speak English find it respectful that all the printed materials are in Spanish.

Major Actions: Meet with manufacturers to assist in creating Spanish communication.

☐   Tactic Number: 164 **Dia de los Muertos es muy importante**

Tactic: Celebrate the various Hispanic holidays.

Rationale: Days such as Day of the Dead and Cinco de Mayo are important holidays to some Hispanics. Be sure to cover a variety of holidays, and not just Mexican or Puerto Rican holidays.

Major Actions: Meet with the various Hispanic-American groups in your community. If you don't have such a group, you may not want to consider this target market.

☐   Tactic Number: 165 **Aviso!**

Tactic: Create a Hispanic advisory board in each of the supermarkets you are targeting Hispanics.

Rationale: There might be local important issues which only members of the community could be aware of.

Major Actions: Be sure to tap your shoppers as well as community leaders.

□ Tactic Number: 166 **Ser un salado**

Tactic: Have Spanish speaking employees in the store.

Rationale: Many Hispanics are embarrassed that they can't speak English and are afraid to ask for help.

Major Actions: In most communities, there are potential employees looking for work. You may need a special training program to help them in the food business.

□ Tactic Number: 167 **Paz de Cristo**

Tactic: Advertise in church bulletins.

Rationale: The church is a very important part of Hispanic life.

Major Actions: Meet with church officials to see how you can advertise in their bulletins.

□ Tactic Number: 168 **Diez y Seis it's a carnival**

Tactic: Sponsor church events and carnivals.

Rationale: This shows you are part of the community, and not just an outsider trying to make a profit off the residents.

Major Actions: Meet with church officials and see how you can support the church events.

□ Tactic Number: 169 **Hola(t) of customers**

Tactic: Be sure to have checkout personnel who can speak Spanish.

Rationale: So many questions come up in the checkout line and non-English speaking shoppers are often embarrassed when they can't answer or don't understand.

☐ Tactic Number: 170 **Papel o plastic?**

Tactic: Be sure to have all store coupons and specials available in Spanish.

Rationale: In many cases, the Hispanic shoppers gets left out of your great saving sales because they can't read the coupons.

Major Actions: Have local Hispanic community members translate your coupon and specials. Meet with the instant coupon vendors and require them to offer the service in Spanish in your Hispanic targeted stores.

☐ Tactic Number: 171 **Taco me on a tour**

Tactic: Offer stores tours on a regular basis with a Spanish speaking tour guide. Have the tour guide explain, not only where the Hispanic foods are, but also how to use all the other non-Hispanic foods in your store.

Rationale: You won't sell the whole store to your Hispanic shoppers unless they know how to use your foods and where to find them.

Major Actions: Ask one of your shoppers in the store to run the stores tours and give them a discount for their efforts.

☐ Tactic Number: 172 **Hard to tapas**

Tactic: Do sampling programs of typically Hispanic foods and Spanish speaking sampling personnel.

Rationale: Hispanics like to try new foods as much as anyone, but foods targeted to them are virtually never sampled.

Major Actions: Be sure to only work with vendors that do sampling that offer Spanish speaking personnel. They may at first balk, but if they want to keep the business they will find the people.

☐   Tactic Number: 173 **Time to Go ya**

Tactic: Be a sponsor of the various events that take place in the Hispanic community. For example, Puerto Rico Day, or other major events.

Rationale: It is important that Hispanics see you as a supporter of all their events not just in the store.

☐   Tactic Number: 174 **Neato bienvenido**

Tactic: Make effort to communicate with newcomers to the Hispanic community. Welcome Wagon is often only in the suburbs.

Rationale: Create your version of a Welcome Wagon.

Major Actions: Create baskets of Hispanic products and coupons with printed material that shows you want Hispanic business and are Hispanic friendly.

☐   Tactic Number: 175 **Out to al pastor**

Tactic: Have a monthly, or at least a regular, Hispanic day in the store. Have Hispanic decorations, and sales on Hispanic foods. Make it an event.

Major Actions: Meet with manufacturers and get their support for each event. One month could be the Coca Cola event, and next month the 3M sponsored event, etc.

☐   Tactic Number: 176 **Salsa and peppers**

Tactic: Have popular Hispanic music playing in the store. This need not be all day or every day, but make Hispanic music a part of the total offering.

Rationale: Every target group likes to hear music of their own group.

Major Actions: Find the local radio stations or have the music vendors supply Hispanic music. Be sure to vary the country of origin.

☐   Tactic Number: 177 **It's chili in here**

Tactic: Offer traditional Hispanic foods in your prepared food or deli section.

Rationale: Hispanic shoppers are as time starved as anyone, and enjoy buying fresh prepared food as much as any group.

Major Actions: Make sure the recipes are original and not Americanized. Try to create a partnership with a Hispanic restaurant.

☐   Tactic Number: 178 **I siesta where to park**

Tactic: Be sure that the outside signage is in Spanish. Handicapped parking, cart return, no parking etc. should all be in Spanish.

Rationale: Some will judge your store before they ever get inside.

☐   Tactic Number: 179 **Not a mole**

Tactic: Create a Hispanic liaison who will be available in the store to help the Hispanic shopper. He/she will also be able to bring problems and issues to management that the shopper would not bring.

Major Actions: This can be a volunteer, or someone who gets a discount. It can be the same person who gives store tours.

☐   Tactic Number: 180 **Honor the hairitage**

Tactic: Have an expanded health and beauty section that includes products targeted to the Hispanic shopper.

Rationale: Hispanics spend disproportionately more on these products than their Anglo counterparts, and use specific products tailored to their needs.

Major Actions: Meet with your suppliers to help design this section.

☐   Tactic Number: 181 **In plantain sight**

Tactic: Have an expanded bulk food section of commodity foods such as flour, rice, beans, sugar and other baking products.

Rationale: Hispanics still cook from scratch and use more of the basic products than other groups.

The
Ethnic Group
Target Market

(Asian)

Tactic Number: 182 **I like me**

Tactic: Install a special section in the in-store books that appeals to the to the Asian-American consumer in the store's trade area. This section could be store run or leased out.

Rationale: research indicates that Asians are fond of reading books on their own culture than "regular" books. Asians as a group are also more loyal to grocery stores than to any other type of retail store.

Major actions: Contact book supplier, or visit Chinatown in major cities, for examples of available books.

Tactic Number: 183 **Very rice!**

Tactic: Create a "store within the store" concept in a market area where there are one or more Asian American ethnic groups. This would be like a marketplace having separate Chinese, Japanese, Korean, Vietnamese and Filipino products that are merchandised to the target market.

Rationale: Most Anglos would know that Asians prefer to eat rice, yet would not be readily aware there are distinct differences in the type of rice various ethnic groups prefer within the Asian market

Major actions: Contact an Asian food supplier. They are very entrepreneurial and would most likely direct store ship or even maintain the sections.

Tactic Number: 184 **Something fishy**

Tactic: Have live fish available, where a customer can choose the fish they want, and you will then prepare it for cooking (or at least kill it).

Rationale: Asians love to choose their fish from live fish displays.

The Older Target Market

Tactic Number: 185 **Exercise never gets old**

Tactic: Give Senior Citizens in-store fitness demos. Get with area fitness experts to put together special fitness programs for the elderly that they will be able to do regularly.

Rationale: Health and fitness are extremely important to older people.

Major Actions: Get with a local health and fitness club to develop an in-store program. The club should find this desirable, since they can look for new members.

Tactic Number: 186 **Better than the rest**

Tactic: Put benches around in the store.

Rationale: Older people need to rest more frequently than other shoppers.

Major Actions: Approach various manufacturers, and ask them to sponsor the bench. Be able to print on the bench, "This seat is provided by the Coca-Cola Company."

Tactic Number: 187 **Oh, now I see**

Tactic: Be sure the shelf labels are in extra large print, and you do a good job of keeping the right labels in front of the right products.

Rationale: Older people have a more difficult time with their vision, and have a little more difficult time associating shelf price tags with products that are not immediately above the tags.

Major Actions: Check with label printers to increase print font sizes.

Tactic Number: 188 **All the right ingredients**

Tactic: Create recipe books of the recipes created by the older shoppers within the store.

Rationale: Many of the older shoppers have years and years of experience, and have discovered many wonderful recipes which they have used. Create a cookbook of recipes from just people from around store. The cookbook can be chain wide.

Major Actions: Invite older shoppers to send in recipes at checkout, and get support from the manufacturers since many recipes will use branded products.

☐ Tactic Number: 189 **It's the Buick**

Tactic: Have staff available to carry the bags of older people to their cars.

Rationale: Many older people have a difficult time carrying heavy packages.

Major Actions: Be sure to do a small study to find when most of your older shoppers are in the store.

☐ Tactic Number: 190 **Big band party**

Tactic: Run a shuttle bus from the various retirement communities in your area. Bring the customers to the store all together, and make an event out of shopping.

Rationale: Older people frequently have a more difficult time with transportation.

Major Actions: Be sure to consider the possibility of having someone on the shuttle bus actually carry the bags from the bus to their front door.

☐ Tactic Number: 191 **Respect**

Tactic: Have sensitivity training programs for your employees, so they anticipate some of the problems that older people will have in their stores. For example, if they see an older person struggling with a package on a high shelf, make sure they understand they should not wait for the person to ask for assistance, but immediately, unsolicited go to help.

Rationale: Many older people don't want to ask for help. Give them assistance before they must ask.

☐ Tactic Number: 192 **No waste for your waist**

Tactic: Keep a wide variety of single serving products, especially in produce, where products should be able to be purchased in the smallest possible quantities.

Rationale: Older people frequently eat less than other groups, and oftentimes are more likely to be a single person household. They don't need the larger quantities that are available.

☐ Tactic Number: 193 **Coffee me now!**

Tactic: Create a Senior Citizen morning shopping event.

Rationale: There are often mornings (Monday, Tuesday) when the store is not particularly busy. It's an opportunity to bring in Senior Citizens, and provide some special benefits which you might not want to do every day.

Major Actions: Offer a coffee hour, possibly have places for people to sit, have newspapers available for people to read. Make coming to the store an enjoyable occasion, and while you are here, shop.

☐ Tactic Number: 194 **Swingin' in the cereal aisle**

Tactic: Play music in the store that is reminiscent of the era of the people that are in the store. On Senior Citizen event days, have music from the 30s or the 40s.

Rationale: Seniors love music from their era, and they hear so little of it today.

Major Actions: Contact the in-store radio supplier or have a committee of shoppers create a mix to be played at specific times.

Tactic Number: 195 **It's the little old lady from produce**

Tactic: Have electric carts for older people to drive around.

Rationale: Mobility is a difficult problem for many older people.

Major Actions: Ask manufacturers who make products that are particularly pertinent to older people to have sponsorship of some of these carts.

Tactic Number: 196 **Express concern**

Tactic: Have older person express checkout lanes.

Rationale: Older people seem particularly irritated about waiting, and in many cases tire quickly standing in line. Have a line where they can go to check out quickly, whether they have 10 items or 100 items. Make it available for them.

Major Actions: It works for airlines, it can work in supermarkets.

Tactic Number: 197 **Where is it????**

Tactic: Have easily accessible bathrooms that are well marked.

Rationale: Older people frequently have various incontinence problems, and require a more frequent use of the bathroom. However, they don't enjoy having to walk around asking everyone where the bathrooms are. Make them visible and clean.

Major Actions: Visit Walmart and see how it is done.

Tactic Number: 198 **A healthy age**

Tactic: Offer special nutrition services for healthy eating for the elderly.

Rationale: The elderly are particularly sensitive to issues related to food and health. And at the same time, have many health issues which are truly related to nutrition and their health.

Major Actions: Have one of the manufacturers sponsor a seminar on the mornings of the Senior Citizen event days, to explain to them basic issues.

☐ Tactic Number: 199 **A wheeled meal**

Tactic: Offer to deliver the foods to the home, rather than have the older people take them home.

Rationale: In many cases, it is difficult for older people to get to and from the store. And even though they might be able to get to the store, they would have difficulty getting their packages home.

Major Actions: Contact "Meals on Wheels", or local taxi service, to supply delivery service.

☐ Tactic Number: 200 **You move me**

Tactic: Permit older people to call and place orders by telephone. Of course, have the home delivery that goes with this.

Rationale: The mobility problem of older people makes it difficult for them to get to the store.

Major Actions: Put brochures at checkout to announce the service. Encourage the staff to distribute when bagging.

☐ Tactic Number: 201 **Eye see**

Tactic: Offer health-related services within the supermarket on a regular basis. For instance, blood pressure screening, eye testing, cholesterol checks, etc.

Rationale: Older people like to go to places where they can have many of these health tests monitored.

Major Actions: Be sure, if you offer these services, they are always available. Many of the machines available in drugstores today do not work.

☐   Tactic Number: 202 **Back then, minimum wage was….**

Tactic: Hire as many part time older people as possible, to be within the store.

Rationale: Seniors always feel more comfortable in the company of their peers, as do any other cohort group.

Major Actions: Make it a Human Resources priority, or it won't get done.

☐   Tactic Number: 203 **People helping people**

Tactic: Establish a roving "senior helper". Have a Senior Citizen roaming through the store, helping Seniors, asking if there is anything else the store can do, and make it clear that this person is there to assist the Senior Citizens in their daily shopping activities.

Rationale: In many cases, older people are embarrassed to say that they are a little confused with all the changes that are taking place in the world, and of course within the store. This person can go up to them, they are a peer, and make sure that everything is going well.

Major Actions: Since many older people want to help their peers, you may create a volunteer service and give the volunteers store discounts, rather than have them as store employees.

☐   Tactic Number: 204 **Help in any way you cane**

Tactic: Offer weekly or monthly Senior Orientation days, where Seniors would be given a store tour and have all the new items in the store explained to them. Provide them with the coupons that will be available in that week's circular, and tell them all the specials that will be available during the week. Provide coffee and some kind of enjoyable social occasion.

Rationale: Seniors are less adventuresome. The orientation would help them explore the entire store.

Major Actions: Create a position of Senior Citizen Coordinator.

☐   Tactic Number: 205 **What's old is new again**

Tactic: Offer special sampling occasions for Senior Citizens on Senior Citizen event days.

Rationale: Senior Citizens may be a little bit more reluctant to try new products and new things since they may feel "set in their ways." Be a little more aggressive in offering them new products, rather than waiting for Seniors to try them.

Major Actions: Use your database to find out what older people are buying the most and the least, as a basis for sampling.

☐   Tactic Number: 206 **Available on all continence**

Tactic: Have an expanded health care section specifically targeted to products that may have higher use among the elderly.

Rationale: Older Americans spend more than average on this category.

Major Actions: Be careful to have a respectful display, and not make it look demeaning.

☐   Tactic Number: 207 **Rack 'em and stack 'em**

Tactic: Have an employee available walking up and down the checkout aisles to assist Senior Citizens in putting their food items on the conveyor belt, not just helping them bag the items.

Rationale: Some of the packages are particularly heavy for the Senior Citizens.

Major Actions: Be sure to do this proactively, and not to wait until someone must ask. Again, that is frequently embarrassing and demeaning.

☐   Tactic Number: 208 **Pill out all the stops**

Tactic: Supermarkets with drugstores should offer reminder services for the elderly as their prescriptions are about to run out. Possibly a telephone call, or a postcard, saying, "Your prescription should be getting low."

Rationale: We all get more forgetful as we age.

Major Actions: Consider using an automated telephone system that automatically sends reminders.

☐   Tactic Number: 209 **All in this together**

Tactic: For supermarkets with drugstores, the druggist should call the older people on some regular basis (once every couple of months would be enough), to find out if they are having any problem with any of the medicines they are taking and just to ask if everything is going well.

Rationale: Many older people become complacent about taking their medicine, or in many cases, forget to take their medicine. Or they don't understand some of the instructions with their medicine.

Major Actions: Get pharmaceutical companies involved. The branded companies are always looking for ways to differentiate themselves from the generics.

☐   Tactic Number: 210 **Edsel Parking Only**

Tactic: Reserve several parking spaces close to the front door for our older people.

Rationale: Older people driving to the store may not have mobility problems, but it gives them more prestige in having a parking space close to the store.

Major Actions: Give decals in the store. Call them special customers, not old customers.

☐ Tactic Number: 211 **That sale never gets old**

Tactic: Be sure to offer sales or promotions in the weekly circular, on products that are targeted to older people.

Rationale: In many cases, older people believe they are just a second thought. By demonstrating that products they consume more regularly are on sale, or promoted, or listed in the circular, it shows you really care about them.

☐ Tactic Number: 212 **Many hands make light work**

Tactic: During evening hours, be sure to offer Senior Citizens an escort to the car.

Rationale: Even though you may perceive the parking lots to be very safe, issues of safety are very much a concern of older people. The offer to escort them to the car may in fact be greatly appreciated. Again, this must be done discreetly and respectfully or it will be a failure.

Major Actions: Be sure to have extra staff available.

☐ Tactic Number: 213 **Let me help you there**

Tactic: Special training programs should be provided to all employees to make them aware of the special needs of Senior Citizens, and equally importantly, how to serve those needs respectfully.

Rationale: Many employees are impatient with older shoppers.

☐ Tactic Number: 214 **Hello, Ethel**

Tactic: On Senior Citizen events days, be sure to have name tags with both the names of all the Senior Citizens, and where they are from.

Rationale: They are always looking for ways to strike up conversations with other Seniors, and name tags makes it much easier.

The Teenager Target Market

☐ Tactic Number: 215 **Picture this**

Tactic: Promote picture duplicate processing when proms, formals and class trips take place.

Rationale: Families, as well as teens, take pictures during those times. Although they are on their handhelds, many want hard copies.

Major Actions: Give deals to those with prom tickets, or trip receipts

☐ Tactic Number: 216 **Eight inches of space, please**

Tactic: Sponsor store dance parties in parking lot on weekends during summer months

Rationale: Gets teens familiar with the store location, and you will sell snacks and related products the night of the dance

Major Actions: Have local DJs play music and try to co-sponsor with Coke or Pepsi

☐ Tactic Number: 217 **Put down the Twinkies**

Tactic: Give In-store nutrition programs for numerous school groups such as sport teams, weight control as well as Home Economics.

Rationale: These classes don't get the attention of school administration, and the teachers would be very grateful.

Major Actions: Find co-sponsors such as Weight Watchers, Gatorade, Pillsbury

☐ Tactic Number: 218 **This is what we call a frying pan**

Tactic: Be an aggressive participant in Home Economics programs, including in-store shopping trips, coupons for products being used in class, and delivery to the school.

Rationale: These kids are being taught to use the products you sell. Get them to know where they can get them.

Major Actions: Contact Home Economics teacher.

☐ Tactic Number: 219 **Driving me crazy**

Tactic: Be aggressive sponsors of teen-oriented causes, such as SADD, drug awareness, driving safety programs or the homeless.

Rationale: Teens respect people that show respect for their causes.

Major Actions: Find out local causes from your teen shoppers.

☐ Tactic Number: 220 **Nothing but net**

Tactic: Sponsor school events such as Homecoming Queen or Athlete of the Week.

Rationale: These events are often more important to the parents than the teens.

Major Actions: Bring him/her to the store for pictures and PR.

☐ Tactic Number: 221 **You play like a girl**

Tactic: Sponsor girls' sports teams

Rationale: The boys get much more attention, and the girls are not only a better target market, they will be appreciative of the sponsorship.

Major Actions: Contact women's coaches.

☐ Tactic Number: 222 **Chip in a discount**

Tactic: Run teen promotions, for example show school ID card and get a special price on store made pizzas, CSDs, or other snacks. Advertise promotion in school news. Make offer good with student ID.

Rationale: Teens love special deals.

Major Actions: Find co-sponsors such as Frito-Lay, or Coke.

☐   Tactic Number: 223 **Snap this**

Tactic: Add contemporary signage around teen categories.

Rationale: Teens are bombarded with flash. Make them feel at home with your store signs.

Major Actions: Don't offend other shoppers with the signs. They don't have to like them, just not offended by them.

☐   Tactic Number: 224 **Who's Elvis?**

Tactic: Have more current music on the in-store radio during hours when teens are more likely to be present, such as 3-5 PM, or later at night on weekends

Rationale: Teens enjoy teen music.

Major Actions: Ensure the music doesn't offend other shoppers. It doesn't have to be their favorite, just not offend. Shouldn't be extreme. There are compromises.

☐   Tactic Number: 225 **Loafing in the bakery**

Tactic: Create a teen entertainment area including video games. Make area to sit and socialize.

Rationale: This is the gaming generation.

Major Actions: Try to co-sponsor with Call of Duty or Fortnite.

☐   Tactic Number: 226 **An eating teen is a happy teen**

Tactic: Offer catering service for school-related events, such as pre-prom and post prom parties. Be sure foods are teen favorites, not adult favorites. Include teen party planning advice.

Rationale: Teens frequently party, and two income households can't find time to plan.

Major Actions: Cooperate with SADD, and driving safety programs, on party advice.

☐ Tactic Number: 227 **I'm board**

Tactic: Create a teen advisory board to provide input as to how to make store more teen friendly, as well as how to better deal with shoplifting.

Rationale: No one knows more about teens than teens.

Major Actions: Have meetings of all store boards at a nice location once a year.

☐ Tactic Number: 228 **So money possibilities**

Tactic: Participate in school fund raising programs for school trips, band uniforms, etc.

Rationale: Fund raising is a regular school activity

Major Actions: Let the teens use parking lot for car washing projects. Let them sell Coke, and snacks to those waiting, to raise additional money. Let them collect paper, cans etc. for resale.

☐ Tactic Number: 229 **Food fight!**

Tactic: Create a teen theme food court.

Rationale: Teens use meal occasions as social occasions.

Major Actions: Be sure to include teen favorite foods, from pizza to your bakery foods.

☐ Tactic Number: 230 **No ads!**

Tactic: Add deals on Spotify and Pandora to your offer.

Rationale: Teens spend a significant amount on these products.

☐ Tactic Number: 231 **Be prepared**

Tactic: Stock easy to prepare foods in a special section called "teen dinners" such as shelf stable, and microwavable meals. Make them teen favorites.

Rationale: Teens are more than ever responsible for preparing their own meals.

Major Actions: Use a teen advisory board, to find the right foods.

☐ Tactic Number: 232 **Snack peak**

Tactic: Stock fresh prepared, and immediately consumable foods, in an "after school snack" section.

Rationale: Teens eat constantly, and therefore buy food right after school.

☐ Tactic Number: 233 **Smells like teen spirit**

Tactic: Create a teen personal care section. Stock a wide variety of teen personal care products. Include all the teen targeted products such as Teen Spirit deodorant.

Rationale: Teens spend more on personal care than food.

Major Actions: Use special displays and signs to get attention. Ask a leading manufacturer for assistance.

⊓ Tactic Number: 234 **What a Prom otion**

Tactic: Have an "After the Prom Breakfast".

Rationale: Senior proms are a major event in a teenager's life, and everyone usually goes out all night and goes around for different breakfasts. Set up an entire location where eggs and ham and breakfast can be made and provided for the teenagers.

Major Actions: Meet with school officials to work out details.

⊓ Tactic Number: 235 **Full send!**

Tactic: Have amateur nights for various entertainment groups. For example, high school bands, comedians and other talents. These could be held in the parking lot, and could be made into an evening for the teenagers.

Rationale: Not only will teens buy food for the events, but their parents become familiar with your store.

Major Actions: Ask school officials for assistance.

⊓ Tactic Number: 236 **That's a lot**

Tactic: Offer your parking lot for fund raising car washes.

Rationale: Neighborhood groups such as Boy Scouts, church young people's groups, various high school booster clubs are looking for opportunities to be able to have fund raisers such as car washes.

Major Actions: Keep in mind, the purpose of these activities is not necessarily to immediately make a profit, but to demonstrate that you are a part of their community. You should also note that many of the supplies for the car washing, as well as the towels, the sodas, the snacks etc. these people will probably be buying from your store.

Tactic Number: 237 **Influencer search**

Tactic: Have parking lot star search contests, which permit teenagers to come in and sing, dance, rock bands etc. to emulate the talent search that we see on television or YouTube. Put a theater marquis over ads, pictures of movie stars along marquis aspect of your star search.

Rationale: Teens need opportunities to show off, and of course their parents will be there.

Major Actions: Contact a Public Relations agency to orchestrate the event. Repeat the same event at different schools, to reduce the initial set up costs.

Tactic Number: 238 **Two weeks or a Fortnite**

Tactic: Have gaming contests at the store. Create an event in the parking lot.

Rationale: Video games are major teen interest, and supermarkets have not cashed in on the trend.

The College Student Target Market

Tactic Number: 239 **Caffeine Corner**

Tactic: Offer extended hours during final exams.

Rationale: This is a stressful period for any college student. Many student stay up all hours of the night pouring over their notes and textbooks. To break the tension, many students like to take study breaks. Staying open late will attract students who very frequently eat during these breaks.

Major Actions: Consider also offering such things as coffee, soda, donuts and pizza. Students will come for these things, and they very well may end up buying additional items. Even if they do not, you still have made a positive impression on them. Be sure to advertise in school papers that you have extended hours.

Tactic Number: 240 **Don't go dorm ant**

Tactic: Place coupons in the college welcome kits.

Rationale: Many schools give out shoebox-sized welcome kits for incoming freshmen. By placing coupons, flyers, etc. in this kit, you can begin to establish a relationship that may last throughout the student's years at school.

Major Actions: Contact the local university's student affairs officer.

Tactic Number: 241 **Have a ball**

Tactic: Buy season tickets for local college basketball and football games, and give them away in a contest. Every time a student buys something (and shows student ID), he or she can be entered in a raffle to win a pair of tickets for one game.

Rationale: Often these tickets are for sold out events. Therefore, they become very valuable. By giving them away, you show the students that you are willing to give them something desirable to attract their business. If the game is "big", enough students just may be willing to make that extra trip to the store so that they can have their name entered in the contest.

Major Actions: Contact the school's athletic or ticket office to get season tickets. Try to negotiate free advertising in the sports program.

☐   Tactic Number: 242 **It's Kool Aid, I swear**

Tactic: Offer specials for "Tailgaters."

Rationale: Much of the student body (and alumni) turn out before the home games of their teams at many schools. Barbecuing and the consumption of food are among the rituals of tailgating (along with the consumption of beer). Offering specials on your products, and encouraging the students to "stock up" for the tailgate, is a terrific way to build your business.

Major Actions: Advertise in the University paper and Alumni magazine.

☐   Tactic Number: 243 **Just chicken on you**

Tactic: Offer specials before the "big game."

Rationale: If a school's team is in a big game, the students very likely will view the sporting event as one of the great social gatherings of their college life. Many students or student groups throw big parties, where they gather and watch the game. Consider giving away a special prize, such as a color TV for the fraternity or sorority who buys the most amount of hamburgers, hot-dogs, potato chips, beer, and soda etc.

Major Actions: Create the "Sugar Bowl" or "Cotton Bowl" special.

☐   Tactic Number: 244 **Flounder's in seafood again**

Tactic: Sponsor contests among fraternities and sororities.

Rationale: If you organize a contest in which the fraternity and/or sorority who buys the most products wins such things as an iPhone or television, you can build your business. Offer them products which are desirable, and for which they will be willing to compete. You could even post the totals in the front of the store. Make the final presentation a big deal, then take pictures and hang them in your store.

Major Actions: Contact the college administrator for Greek life.

☐   Tactic Number: 245 **Burning hot sale**

Tactic: Have a special promotion on sun screen products in late February or early March.

Rationale: The end of February, and all of March, are traditional times for the college "Spring Break." Many students take this time off and go on a vacation somewhere in the sun.

Major Actions: Help them to prepare by giving special discounts on sun screen products. Consider offering special discounts on other products, which will appeal to spring breakers. This can be an effective way to draw students into your store.

☐   Tactic Number: 246 **What homework?**

Tactic: Sponsor events such as "Spring Fling" or "Greek Week" at the local college.

Rationale: These are events which are traditionally well attended by the student body, because they are fun. You will be associating your name with a fun event. This is an excellent way to make a good impression.

Major Actions: Find out what type of specials would be the most appropriate.

Tactic Number: 247 **We're out of toilet paper?**

Tactic: Offer back to school specials.
Rationale: Grade schoolers are not the only ones who have to worry about getting school supplies. College students need all the same pens, notebooks, paper, etc.

Major Actions: Find out what college students take back to school. It might be quite different from the elementary schoolers. You can also offer "stock up your pantry" specials for college students just moving into apartments.

Tactic Number: 248 **Off the payroll**

Tactic: Give away such things as fruit baskets, flowers, etc. to students who have received job offers.

Rationale: The goal of most college students is to find a job upon graduation. By offering some token of congratulations, you show that you want to recognize and reward the newly employed student.

Major Actions: Post signs that tell students to bring in their offer letters to receive a special gift.

Tactic Number: 249 **Don't tee'se me**

Tactic: Sponsor T-shirts of student groups.

Rationale: Many groups like to get T-shirts made up to announce and/or commemorate their events. To help to reduce their costs, they typically seek local sponsors to put their name on the back of the shirt. This is an excellent way to get recognition, as hundreds of these shirts are typically distributed and worn by the student body for months and years to come.

Major Actions: Contact the college student life office.

☐ Tactic Number: 250 **Metal straws in aisle 8**

Tactic: Stress the fact that your store is environmentally friendly.

Rationale: College is a time when many students leave home for the first time. They are exposed to many new and different ideas. Frequently college students begin to champion social causes, such as the desire for a cleaner environment.

Major Actions: Get the manufacturers of such products to be co-sponsors.

☐ Tactic Number: 251 **A lasting memory**

Tactic: Sponsor such events as STD or SADD awareness programs.

Rationale: For better or worse, many young adults begin to become sexually active when they reach the college years. STDs, and their implications, are important issues for most college students. Sponsoring such programs shows that you care about their health and well-being. Be careful, however, that you do not alienate your other target markets by offending them.

Major Actions: Contact the local sponsoring groups.

☐ Tactic Number: 252 **No means no**

Tactic: Become a champion of social issues which effect college students. Sponsor speakers to come onto campus and lecture about such topics as date rape and on campus violence.

Rationale: Today's college students are faced with growing up in a world full of violence and peril. Show that you are compassionate and are taking an interest in their safety and future.

Major Actions: Contact the local police department or school security office.

Tactic Number: 253 **A major sale**

Tactic: Advertise on the college news site.

Rationale: College students read their campus news sites. It is often suggested to them that they should support those organizations which support their school. A clever ad which announces something which appeals to college students is a great way for you to drum up business in this segment.

Major Actions: Contact the school media.

Tactic Number: 254 **Psychology of snacking 101**

Tactic: Promote your snack section all semester.

Rationale: The college years are filled with snacking at all hours of the night. Take "campus bucks", if your POS system can handle them.

Tactic Number: 255 **A peer appears**

Tactic: Hire students and offer part-time employment with flexible hours.

Rationale: Young people like to shop where their friends work. Also, by offering flexible hours, you will be building a sense of goodwill among students as many have varying schedules.

Major Actions: Advertise on the school media sites for part-time help, or use the bulletin boards in the academic departments.

Tactic Number: 256 **When to say when**

Tactic: If your store sells beer or liquor, extol the virtues of socially responsible drinking. Make it clear that you care about the college students in your area. Show that you are concerned with balancing the sake of their well-being and safety along with their need to have fun.

Rationale: This is a major university and social problem.

☐ Tactic Number: 257 **Alpha Bits Omega**

Tactic: Sponsor community events organized by student groups. Fraternities and sororities are a good example of such groups.

Rationale: A good proportion of college students belong to Greek organizations. Often, they feel as though people in the community have a negative impression of them. By sponsoring some of their charity events on or off campus, you show that you welcome their business.

Major Actions: Contact the university's Greek Life office

☐ Tactic Number: 258 **Better than being in class**

Tactic: Sponsor a college day. Make it fun for them to shop. You could offer such things as a shopping spree for the lucky college student.

Rationale: Students (they believe) have great time constraints and would appreciate anything to make food shopping fun, rather than another drudgery.

☐ Tactic Number: 259 **Eggcellent job, Devils!**

Tactic: Display banners, posters, etc. from the local university.

Rationale: Students like to feel that local businesses are loyal to their school. This is why many bars and fast food restaurants prominently display such items.

Major Actions: Contact the admissions office.

☐ Tactic Number: 260 **Cash me outside**

Tactic: Offer check cashing services.

Rationale: Many college students live away from home where they do their banking. Offering to cash checks from their part-time jobs will appeal to them. This will save them the hassle of opening a local account.

☐ Tactic Number: 261 **Grade A deal**

Tactic: Offer discounts to students who show college ID.

Rationale: A large portion of a college student's disposable income is spent on food. Since they are typically on a tight budget, an across the board discount will appeal to these students.

☐ Tactic Number: 262 **Filler up**

Tactic: Offer inexpensive meals like fried chicken, which appeal to college students. Consider having a "value meal" which would include side dishes and a beverage.

Rationale: The typical college student is on a tight budget and is looking for "cheap food" which will fill him or her up.

Major Actions: Look at some of the fast food "value meals" for examples.

The Upscale Target Market

☐ Tactic Number: 263 **Finnish your plate**

Tactic: Have international food festivals, where foods from all over the world are put on sale. For example, you could have cheeses from France and Denmark, cookies and crackers from England, pastas, olives and olive oils from Italy, seafood from Japan and Norway, imported teas and coffee etc.

Rationale: Many of the upscale have in fact traveled and eaten these foods all over the world, and it is a chance to show them that you appreciate they have a wider experience with foods than many people.

Major Actions: Consider making this a tent event, which would create more excitement with having people in local costumes and maybe even food prepared. Certainly, you can contact the German-American society, etc. to get them to participate in these events.

☐ Tactic Number: 264 **Weight a minute**

Tactic: Hire a full-time nutritionist to work in your store.

Rationale: Upscale shoppers are among the most health conscious.

Major Actions: This nutritionist can assist with planning healthy recipes, weight-loss programs, and answering questions in general.

☐ Tactic Number: 265 **The purrfect pet aisle**

Tactic: Take extra care to see that your store is sparkling clean and meticulously merchandised. Consider upgrading your fixtures in these stores.

Rationale: Image and appearance often are more important to the upscale shopper than price. But don't overdo it, no one wants to think they are paying higher prices for fancy interiors.

Tactic Number: 266 **A good brass kicking**

Tactic: Add attractive display cases to improve the appearance of your store.

Rationale: Perception precedes price with the upscale customer, and one of the problems with most supermarkets is that they are dull and unattractive.

Major Actions: Consider customized shelving with brass and mahogany.

Tactic Number: 267 **I've bin there**

Tactic: Rather than simply offering a candy aisle, consider having a separate section for sweets and chocolate.

Rationale: This could be a store within a store.

Major Actions: Offer free samples of exotic chocolates and candies. This will make impulse buying of candy more likely. Consider making different varieties of fudge in your store.

Tactic Number: 268 **Full steam ahead**

Tactic: Have large tanks of live lobsters and fish. Give your customers a reason to shop in your store, rather than a seafood market.

Rationale: This eye-catching tank will appeal to the upscale shopper.

Major Actions: Your seafood supplier should be able to provide you with leads for live fish and lobster.

Tactic Number: 269 **Water you looking at?**

Tactic: Consider placing a fountain at the entrance of your produce section.

Rationale: Although it may take up valued space, it will create an atmosphere of excitement. It is an eye appealing and pleasant way to welcome shoppers to your produce department.

Major Actions: Consider surrounding the dancing waters with plants and flowers as well as spot lights which change the color of the water.

☐ Tactic Number: 270 **De livery is waiting**

Tactic: Offer a home delivery service on specialty, gourmet, or exotic items.

Rationale: While it may not be feasible to deliver all your SKUs, you can deliver those products that make your store special.

☐ Tactic Number: 271 **The feast lane**

Tactic: Hire a chef to prepare gourmet meals as an alternative to ordinary store cooked takeout dinners.

Rationale: Upscale consumers want the convenience of high quality food at home.

Major Actions: Consider making these takeout dinners made to order.

☐ Tactic Number: 272 **Leaf it outside**

Tactic: Landscape the outside of your store.

Rationale: The outside appearance of your store says a lot about what is inside. Landscaping, and making the outside aesthetically appealing, will impress your target market.

Major Actions: Contact a local landscaper for ideas that would appeal to your target market. Offer to let them put signage outside the store for reduced costs of maintenance.

☐ Tactic Number: 273 **You're write for me**

Tactic: Send a thank you letter once a year.

Rationale: Distinguish yourself from other stores by personally telling your customers how much you appreciate their business. This need not be restricted to only upscale shoppers.

Major Actions: Hand write, or at least hand sign, the letters, express thanks for the past year and continued service for the next.

☐ Tactic Number: 274 **Mochi animal crackers aisle 2**

Tactic: Have each corner of your store be a specialty area. Be sure to carry products that main stream stores wouldn't have.

Rationale: Give your customers a reason to shop at your store, by distinguishing it from other "plain stores."

Major Actions: One corner could be a candy store, another could be a coffee shop, a third could be a florist, a fourth could be a bank. You are only limited by your imagination.

☐ Tactic Number: 275 **I've bean here before**

Tactic: Place a fresh juice and/or espresso bar near the deli department.

Rationale: Your customers can purchase fresh squeezed juice or espresso/cappuccino, while waiting for their order.

Major Actions: There are many coffee companies that would lease space for this purpose.

☐ Tactic Number: 276 **Remember bake in the day?**

Tactic: Don't just offer gourmet foods, offer gourmet cooking classes, as well.

Rationale: Your customers are spending a great deal of money to buy these products, show them you appreciate their business by showing them delicious and exciting ways to prepare meals. Cooking classes will help your customers enhance their cooking skills and to learn new recipes as well.

Major Actions: Contact a local restaurant chef.   Also, look for "out of work" chefs that might be interested in part time work.

Tactic Number: 277 **Hey, one sample per person!**

Tactic: Institute a policy of regular sampling.

Rationale: Many of the products offered to your customers may be expensive. Free samples will allow them to see for themselves the product is worth the price.

Major Actions: Contact demo companies for scheduling.

Tactic Number: 278 **Filet a gap in the market**

Tactic: Promote a "Butcher Shop" concept.

Rationale: Shoppers can go anywhere and find a meat department.   Be sure to recognize this section is partly for marketing purposes, not just a profit center.

Major Actions: Distinguish your store by offering the finest cuts, along with a service philosophy i.e. cuts made to order etc.

Tactic Number: 279 **Now stay right here**

Tactic: Provide an entertainment area where kids can go and play and be supervised, while their parents shop.

Rationale: Many children find it boring to go food shopping. Rather than making the shopping trip unpleasant (and probably shorter) for the parent, offer them this service.

Tactic Number: 280 **Hello, my name is**

Tactic: Offer an order ahead service where your customers can place their orders ahead of time.

Rationale: This will save your customers time, and it is an excellent way to communicate with them.

Major Actions: Advertise this service in you weekly circular.

☐   Tactic Number: 281 **How do you spell Porsche?**

Tactic: Offer custom decorating of birthday cakes in your bakery.

Rationale: Upscale customers are willing to pay a little more for services such as these. This will be a more appealing cake than a generic happy birthday, congratulations, etc.

☐   Tactic Number: 282 **Where's my Beemer?**

Tactic: Keep your parking lot spotless and well lit.

Rationale: A dirty, dimly lit parking lot will be a huge turnoff to the upscale shopper (or really any shopper).

☐   Tactic Number: 283 **They'll loave you**

Tactic: Offer homemade rye breads, bobka, strudels, etc. in your bakery department.

Rationale: Upscale breads for upscale shoppers.

Major Actions: Make sure the pleasant aroma of your bakery is piped into the supermarket. This will please your customers and increase impulse purchases of your bakery products.

☐   Tactic Number: 284 **Great deal on Macintosh apples**

Tactic: Offer in-house credit cards, or Apple Pay, to your customers.

Rationale: Upscale customers usually have less time to shop, and this service will help to make checkout quicker and easier.

Tactic Number: 285 **Champagne wishes**

Tactic: Offer made-to-order party platters with shrimp platters, lobster, caviar, pate, etc., as well as the traditional foods.
Rationale: Most store delis offer party platters, but you can win the upscale customer over by offering something special.

Major Actions: Order some party trays from upscale caterers to get ideas for your trays. Be sure to specially train the people making these trays.

Tactic Number: 286 **Caviar dreams**

Tactic: Offer a complete selection of gourmet cookbooks.

Rationale: There are many exciting and tantalizing gourmet dishes which your customers may be unaware of, or uncertain as to how best to prepare them. Win them over with gourmet cookbooks.

Major Actions: Contact a book distributor for ideas for this section.

Tactic Number: 287 **Gift in line!**

Tactic: Offer an expanded gift section, and consider cross merchandising with greeting cards.

Rationale: Upscale customers often have time pressures and having a well-stocked gift section will make life easier. Yes, people still buy greeting cards.

Tactic Number: 288 **Sales rose last week**

Tactic: Offer a full-service floral department in your store.

Rationale: Upscale shoppers are most likely to purchase flowers. Why make them go to a florist when they can buy flowers and gifts at your store?

☐ Tactic Number: 289 **Let's wok around**

Tactic: Hire a Chinese cook to prepare authentic Chinese dinners.

Rationale: If you offer genuine Chinese food which tastes great, you can lure customers to your store instead of having them go to a local Chinese take-out restaurant.

☐ Tactic Number: 290 **Clean and green**

Tactic: Offer organic products in your store.

Rationale: Upscale consumers are more willing to pay a little extra to try something new.

The Inner City Target Market

Tactic Number: 291 **A clean sweep**

Tactic: Sponsor anti-graffiti campaigns and cleanups.

Rationale: A cleaner surrounding area will make your store more appealing and pleasant to shop in, and shows commitment to the community.

Major Actions: Consider allowing local kids to paint a mural on the side of your building. Use branded cleaning products and get the manufacturer to co-sponsor.

Tactic Number: 292 **An omni bus plan**

Tactic: Offer a shuttle to and from your store.

Rationale: Many of your clientele do not have their own transportation. Their only alternative may be public transportation or shopping at small neighborhood markets.

Tactic Number: 293 **Safety first**

Tactic: Hire security guards.

Rationale: Let your customers feel safe and secure inside and outside your store. Make sure that it is known that the added security is there for their safety, and not to "spy" on them.

Major Actions: Dress them in store uniforms or street clothes not like a police force. Post signs that state the store is protected by security.

Tactic Number: 294 **Light the way**

Tactic: Make sure your parking lot is well lit.

Rationale: Your customers will feel safer outside your store at night if there is brighter lighting in your parking lot.

Tactic Number: 295 **Dietary supplements**

Tactic: Have extra workers on hand at the beginning of the month.

Rationale: This is the time of the month when welfare checks and EBT come in. Since many of your customers may be on government subsidies, they will appreciate your being in stock during the busy times.

Tactic Number: 296 **Sup**

Tactic: Hire managers of the same ethnic background as the surrounding community.

Rationale: People feel more at home when people they recognize are working in the store.

Tactic Number: 297 **Teamwork makes the dream work**

Tactic: Hire your employees from the local community.

Rationale: Providing employment for the community is an excellent way to build a sense of good will.

Major Actions: Put signs in local churches and on bulletin boards. Use your own circulars.

Tactic Number: 298 **Bank on it**

Tactic: Donate food to the local food bank.

Rationale: Many of your customers may be poor. By donating food to organizations such as the local food bank, you show you are sympathetic to those less fortunate than you. Remember many of these people will not be needy forever.

☐ Tactic Number: 299 **What the Ec**

Tactic: Donate food to school home economic programs.

Rationale: The under-funded inner city schools often will cut spending on "non-academic areas", such as Home Economics. Send your private label products and show them at a young age that these products are as good as the branded products.

Major Actions: Contact the Home Economics teacher.

☐ Tactic Number: 300 **Only fried eggs allowed**

Tactic: Sponsor community programs, such as anti-drugs or anti-violence campaigns.

Rationale: These are issues which face inner city neighborhoods every day. Confront them head on, and take an active interest in your community's wellbeing.

☐ Tactic Number: 301 **No one understands me like me**

Tactic: Hire buyers from the same ethnic background as your local community.

Rationale: These people can better identify with your target market. They will be able to help you better merchandise your store to meet the needs and wants of your customers.

Major Actions: Promote from store level. The people may need additional training, but the payoff will follow.

☐ Tactic Number: 302 **You can cash me**

Tactic: Offer a check cashing service.

Rationale: Many of your customers may be poor and need this service to cash checks. It is also useful for the customers who need to cash social security or payroll checks.

☐ Tactic Number: 303 **Healthy idea**

Tactic: Sponsor a health day where you provide free medical checkups.

Rationale: Many of your poorer customers may have inadequate health care. Sponsoring a health day shows your customers that you are concerned with their wellbeing.

Major Actions: Contact your community health department.

☐ Tactic Number: 304 **All aboard the Scholar Ship**

Tactic: Sponsor a scholarship for students in your community.

Rationale: Stress the importance of education and reward academic excellence. This is an excellent way to build up good will within the community. It will also be good PR, since the scholarships are announce repeatedly in the media.

Major Actions: Contact the local high schools for assistance.

☐ Tactic Number: 305 **Prune the dates**

Tactic: Have an event calendar in your store, which posts specials and upcoming community interest events.

Rationale: This is one way to show you are in touch with events in the community. It is also a good way to notify your customers about upcoming specials.

☐ Tactic Number: 306 **We hoop so**

Tactic: Sponsor activities such as midnight basketball programs in your parking lot.

Rationale: This will help to keep kids off the streets and safe from harm. Any positive impact on the community can only help your store.

Major Actions: Contact local college coaches to supply hoops, coaches and referees.

☐ Tactic Number: 307 **All together now**

Tactic: Sponsor community events such as neighborhood watches.

Rationale: Become an intricate part of the community. Show you want to make the area safer.

Major Actions: Sponsor bright colored T-shirts with your store name on it, for those on neighborhood watch; consider letting your store be a safehaven (similar to the block parent program), where children can come if they feel threatened.

☐ Tactic Number: 308 **You're so salty**

Tactic: Sponsor seminars on eating healthy.

Rationale: Many of your customers may have a lower level of education, and are less aware about issues concerning sodium, cholesterol (etc.).

Major Actions: Contact the local Dairy Council for assistance.

☐ Tactic Number: 309 **You collard me there**

Tactic: Sell store cooked soul / southern food, to be taken home.

Rationale: Give your customers an alternative to fast food restaurants.

Major Actions: Make an event out of it in the parking lot.

☐ Tactic Number: 310 **Urban note**

Tactic: Play music which is appealing to your target market.

Rationale: Be careful to select music which will appeal to some in this segment, but not alienate others.

Major Actions: Smooth jazz might be a good idea.

☐ Tactic Number: 311 **Congradulations!**

Tactic: Have a bulletin board in your store which extols the accomplishments of members of the neighborhood, offers congratulations on weddings, graduations (etc.).

Rationale: Show you take an interest in members of the community, and you want them to be recognized.

☐ Tactic Number: 312 **You're a good sport**

Tactic: Organize group outings to hometown sporting events. Provide transportation.

Rationale: Many of your customers are no doubt sports fans, but cannot get to the stadium unless they use public transportation. You can also get group rates on tickets.

The Weight Conscious Target Market

Tactic Number: 313 **Hey, weight!**

Tactic: Print low fat, low calorie, easy to prepare recipes in your weekly circular (along border, etc.). Coordinate with recipe items on sale that week.

Rationale: Weight conscious people often view losing weight as a chore and need help in figuring out low calorie alternative eating patterns.

Major Actions: Contact the local American Dietetic Association, or the Dairy Council, for low calorie recipes.

Tactic Number: 314 **Producing healthy effects**

Tactic: Have a produce sale targeted to the weight conscious group. In-store circular could provide actual calories of lettuce, carrots, cucumbers, etc. Have everything on sale to make a great salad. Merchandise low fat dressings in produce area.

Rationale: Weight conscious group wants interesting things to eat.

Major Actions: Be sure not to focus on weight, but rather comparing your fresh produce to the other prepared diet foods like Weight Watchers. Compare taste and calorie content.

Tactic Number: 315 **Are you prepared?**

Tactic: Include low fat, low calorie foods in your prepared food deli case.

Rationale: Convenience is as important to the weight conscious group as it is to other groups.

Major Actions: Ask your caterer or supplier to supply low calorie prepared foods.

Tactic Number: 316 **Pizza has how many calories?**

Tactic: Have printed slips available with complete nutritional contents, including calories for all foods, in your deli case for prepared foods.

Rationale: The weight conscious group tends to read labels, but prepared foods typically do not include them, unless mandated by the state.

Major Actions: Suppliers should be able to provide you with the information.

Tactic Number: 317 **Built to scale**

Tactic: Have a scale in a room where customers can record their weekly or monthly weight loss. Reward consumers with a small gift for reaching milestones.

Rationale: Weight watchers are weight watchers.

Major Actions: Contact manufacturers to co-sponsor the room. Be sure its private.

Tactic Number: 318 **Nothing to lose**

Tactic: Sponsor special conscientious weight loss programs in schools for teens with weight problems.

Rationale: Teens have many eating disorders and are obsessed with weight loss. Helping them control their weight in a healthy way endears not only the teens, but their parents as well.

Major Actions: Contact the school nurse or health education teacher.

⊔ Tactic Number: 319 **Buy low cal**

Tactic: Team up with a Weight Watchers group to come in and demonstrate how to make low calorie meals from items in your store.

Rationale: This will benefit Weight Watchers, because they may get more members to sign up and you will get expert advice.

⊔ Tactic Number: 320 **Bro, you chure?**

Tactic: Develop a brochure that can be placed in Weight Watchers offices, or local weight control programs (without their own food), that explains your store is there to serve the complete dietary needs of the weight conscious consumer.

Rationale: Let people who are interested in weight loss know your store caters to their needs.

⊔ Tactic Number: 321 **Die with a T**

Tactic: Put many of the diet books available today in your book or magazine section. Make sure you have a complete source of all the latest literature on diets, dieting and weight loss.

Rationale: Most dieters are voracious readers of these materials.

Major Actions: Be sure to include not just fad diets but many of the more recognized legitimate diets as well.

⊔ Tactic Number: 322 **You butter not**

Tactic: Hold healthy cooking classes, with a dietitian on hand. Show how making your own food at home is the best alternative for healthy eating, and weight loss.

Rationale: Most dieters would love to be in control of their own ingredients in their food, but may not know how to cook.

Conclusion

So, there you have it. Simple solutions requiring no upgrade to your POS system, no major degree in computer science, and only the most important ingredient- you. You. You, and a positive, passionate attitude. You, with your head on straight and an undying desire to share your store with your customers. You, wanting to make your store their store.

That's all the customer has ever wanted anyway!

Made in the USA
Monee, IL
20 December 2019